EXPLANATI...
***

CREED

***

by
Abu Muhammad al-Hasan ibn 'Alee ibn Khalf
al-Barbahaaree
(d.329H) rahimahullaah

Translated by
Abu Talhah Daawood ibn Ronald Burbank

Published by
Al-Haneef Publications,
P.O. Box 3465,
Birmingham,
B10 9AT
United Kingdom

Distribution by
Al-Hidaayah Publishing & Distribution,
P.O. Box 3332,
Birmingham B10 9AW
United Kingdom

Tel: 0121 753 1889
Fax: 0121 753 2422

Printed by All Trade Printers, Birmingham

CONTENTS

$$\text{بِسْمِ اللَّهِ الرَّحْمَنِ الرَّحِيمِ}$$

Publisher's Foreword

All praise is for Allaah, Lord of the worlds, prayers and peace be upon Muhammad (ﷺ), his family, his Companions and all those who follow in his (ﷺ) footsteps until the Last Day.

Before you is an English translation of Imaam al-Barbahaaree's classic work, *Sharh as-Sunnah*. The translation has been based upon the Arabic edition of *Sharh as-Sunnah* produced by Khaalid ar-Radaadee. As well as translating ar-Radaadee's footnotes to the text, Abu Talhah has added further notes using the taped lectures of Shaikh Saaleh as-Suhaimee's explanation of *Sharh as-Sunnah*. Further, Abu Talhah has also made use of excerpts from Muhammad ibn Sa'eed al-Qahtaanee's Arabic edition of *Sharh as-Sunnah*. We have tried to ensure that most of the points of creed mentioned in the book have been backed up by proof but at the same time have tried to keep the book to a reasonable size.

Four appendices have been provided elaborating further some important issues, as well as a subject index and a glossary.

The extensive footnotes should add further authority to the work for one who accepts with full conviction the authority of the Book of Allaah and the Sunnah of the Messenger of Allaah (ﷺ). Ample sayings of the early scholars, reinforce the correctness of what has been said.

We hope, as al-Barbahaaree hoped, that, "Perhaps through it (i.e. this book), Allaah will bring a confused person out of his confusion, or an innovator out of his innovation, or a misguided one out of his misguidance and he may be saved through it."

We hope that Allaah accepts this humble effort and has mercy upon us and you on that Day when everyone will seek His Mercy.

Introduction

Indeed all praise is for Allaah, we praise him, seek His aid and ask for His forgiveness. We seek Allaah's refuge from the evil of ourselves and our evil actions. Whomsoever Allaah guides, he is rightly guided. Whomsoever Allaah misguides, none can guide him. I bear witness that none has the right to be worshipped but Allaah, alone, having no partner and I bear witness that Muhammad is His slave and His Messenger. May Allaah send praises and blessings upon him, his family (and followers) and his Companions. From the completion of Allaah's blessings upon his servants is that He completed this Religion for them. He, the Most High, says:

ٱلۡيَوۡمَ أَكۡمَلۡتُ لَكُمۡ دِينَكُمۡ وَأَتۡمَمۡتُ عَلَيۡكُمۡ نِعۡمَتِى وَرَضِيتُ لَكُمُ ٱلۡإِسۡلَٰمَ دِينًا

This Day have I completed your Religion for you, bestowed my favours upon you and have chosen for you Islaam as your Religion.[1]

The Prophet (ﷺ) was not taken until he had left us upon pure and clear guidance, whose night is like its day and no one deviates from it except that he is destroyed. "Certainly in the beginning this *Ummah* enjoyed Allaah's mercy, as Allaah united it upon guidance and united the hearts of its people and protected it from falling into innovation since it stood firmly upon obedience to Allaah and His Messenger (ﷺ). The Companions of the Prophet (ﷺ) were accustomed only to following him, giving him full honour and following the light which was sent down with him, submitting fully to the truth which he came with. They had no saying along with his saying nor any opposition to his judgement."[2]

---

1. Soorah al-Maai'dah (5):3
2. *Al-'Aqeedatus-Salafiyyah min Kalam Rabbil-Bariyyah* of Shaikh 'Abdullaah al-Judai' (p.9).

Those of the best generations, the *Taabi'een* and those who came after them, the rightly guided *Imaams*, may Allaah be pleased with them all, followed their way and continued upon that path. Later there came generations who, "were not satisfied with Allaah's revelation and His *Sharee'ah*; rather they imagined that there was need for correction, addition and deletion, so they applied their own minds to the perfect Revelation and sought to amend the rulings of the Ever-Living, the Sustainer of everything. So they split up their Religion and became sects and a multitude of paths appeared before the people and there occurred that which the Prophet (ﷺ) had feared for his *Ummah* - leaders of misguidance.... so discord occurred and increased greatly to the point that most of them turned away from the Book, others sought to strike some *Aayaat* against others and to dispute futilely in order to rebut the truth. Iblees made this alluring in their eyes so that they saw it as something good and they thought it to be perfectly rational and correct."[1]

The people of the innovated sects did not desist from hiding the truth and propagating their falsehood until they managed to spread their futile beliefs and innovations by every means possible. But Allaah, the Most High, provided for this Religion scholars who acted upon their knowledge and sincere *Imaams* who repelled from it the accretions and alterations of the innovators, the false claims of the liars and the false interpretations of the ignorant. There has been in every age a noble company of them standing firm and expending great efforts in defending the Book of Allaah and the *Sunnah* of His Messenger (ﷺ) and in refuting the people of innovated beliefs, innovation, deviation and misguidance. At the head of them towards the end of the third century and the beginning of the fourth was the *Imaam* who aided the *Sunnah* and subdued innovation: Abu Muhammad al-Hasan ibn 'Alee al-

---

1. Ibid. p.10-11.

Barbahaaree (d.329H). The *Imaam* expended great efforts in defending the *Sunnah* and the *'Aqeedah* (creed) of *Ahl us-Sunnah wal-Jamaa'ah* and in opposing the armies of deviant sects and the people of innovation. He made clear the false beliefs which they manifested and exposed the evil which they hid.

I came across this important work of the *Imaam*, entitled *Sharh us-Sunnah*. I found it to be very important and valuable. In compiling it, the author followed the way and methodology of the *Salaf* (the Pious Predecessors), asserting the *'Aqeedah* (creed) they held in the light of the Book and the *Sunnah*, bringing attention to and warning against the way of the people of deviant sects and innovation and fully exposing their evil and falsehood. So I was of the view that it was essential to give full attention to it, revise it and publish it, thereby rendering a great service to the *Sunnah* and its people. Therefore, I definitely resolved to do this and also to make a study of the author and his work. This was accomplished and all praise and thanks are for Allaah and all blessings are from Him. I do not forget to give thanks, after thanking Allaah, the Mighty and Majestic, to the noble Shaikh Faalih ibn Naafi' al-Harbee, may Allaah protect and preserve him, for his valuable recommendations and the advice which he gave to me so that the book could appear in the best form possible, if Allaah wills. May Allaah grant him the best reward for his assistance.

I ask Allaah, the Mighty and Majestic, to make it a work that is done purely for Him, seeking only His pleasure and that He guides us to and grants us that which He loves and is pleased with. Our final call is that all praise is for Allaah, Lord of all creation.

Written by Abu Yaasir Khaalid ibn Qaasim ar-Radaadee
25/12/1413H
Al-Madeenah

7

About the Author

His Name, Kunyah and Lineage

He is the *Imaam*, the example, the *mujaahid*, the Shaikh of the Hanbalee scholars and greatest of them in his time: Abu Muhammad al-Hasan ibn 'Alee ibn Khalf al-Barbahaaree - an ascription to Barbahaar which were medicines imported from India.[1]

His Birthplace and Early Life

The references available do not mention anything about his birth or early life but it appears that he was born and brought up in Baghdaad. This is apparent from his fame amongst its general public, not to mention its scholars. Further, al-Barbahaaree sat with a group of the companions of the *Imaam* of *Ahl us-Sunnah wal-Jamaa'ah*, Ahmad ibn Hanbal, *rahimahullaah*. He studied under them and most of them came from Baghdaad as will be explained. This shows that he grew up in an environment of knowledge and adherence to the *Sunnah*. This clearly had a great influence upon his personality.

His Teachers and His Seeking After Knowledge

Al-Barbahaaree was pre-eminent in seeking after knowledge and expended great efforts to attain it. He acquired knowledge from a group of the senior students of Imaam Ahmad ibn Hanbal, except that unfortunately the references available to us only state two of them by name and they are:

(i) Ahmad ibn Muhammad ibn ul-Hajjaaj ibn 'Abdul-'Azeez, Abu Bakr al-Marwazee. The exemplary *Imaam*, scholar and

---

1. Refer to *al-Ansaab* of as-Sam'aanee (1/307) and *al-Jubaab* of Ibn ul-Atheer (1/133).

8

muhaddith, a student of Imaam Ahmad. He died on the sixth of Jumaadal-Oolaa in the year 275H.[1]

(ii) Sahl ibn 'Abdullaah ibn Yunus at-Tusturee, Abu Muhammad. The *Imaam*, worshipper and one known for abstemiousness from this world. Many wise sayings are reported from him and many remarkable happenings. He died in Muharram in the year 283H, at the age of about eighty.[2]

His Knowledge and the Scholars' Praise of Him

Imaam al-Barbahaaree, *rahimahullaah*, was a formidable and imposing *Imaam*, who spoke out with the truth and called to the *Sunnah* and to the following of the narrations. He also had renown and the respect of the ruler. In his gatherings, various circles for the study of *hadeeth*, the narrations and *fiqh* were held. These were attended by many of the scholars of *hadeeth* and *fiqh*.[3]

The scholar Abu 'Abdullaah said, "If you see a person of Baghdaad loving Abul-Hasan ibn Bashshaar and Abu Muhammad al-Barbahaaree then know that he is a person of the *Sunnah*."[4]

His high status is shown by what his student Ibn Battah, *rahimahullaah*, said, "I heard him - meaning al-Barbahaaree, saying when the people were prevented from Hajj: O people! If anyone needs assistance to the level of a hundred thousand *Deenaars* and a hundred thousand *Deenaars* and a hundred thousand *Deenaars* - five times - then I will assist him." Ibn Battah said, "If he wanted it the people would have given it to him."

---

1. His biography can be found in *Taarekh Baghdaad* (4/423), *Tabaqaat ul-Fuqhahaa'* of ash-Sheeraazee (p.170), *Tabaqaat ul-Hanaabilah* (1/56) and *Siyar A'laamin-Nubalaa'* (13/173).

2. His biography can be found in *al-'Ibr* (1/407) and *as-Siyar* (13/330).

3. *Tabaqaat ul-Hanaabilah* (2/44).

4. *Tabaqaat ul-Hanaabilah* (2/58).

As regards the scholars' praise of him then a great deal is reported:

Ibn Abee Ya'laa said, "... Shaikh of the community in his time and the foremost of them in censuring the people of innovation and in opposing them with his hand and tongue and he had renown with the ruler and prominence amongst those of knowledge and he was one of the wise scholars, great and precise memorisers of the texts and the reliable Believers."

Adh-Dhahabee says in al-'Ibar, "... the exemplary scholar, Shaikh of the Hanbalees in 'Iraaq, in speech, action and sticking to what is lawful. He had great renown and total respect..."

Ibn al-Jawzee said, "... He gathered knowledge and abstention from this world (zuhd) ... and was strong against the people of innovation."

Ibn Katheer said, "The abstemious, man of knowledge, the Hanbalee scholar, the admonisher... and he was strict against the people of innovation and sin. He had great standing and was respected by the elite and by the common people."

His Piety and Abstemiousness (Zuhd)

Imaam al-Barbahaaree was known for both of these qualities. This can be seen by what Abul-Hasan ibn Bashshaar mentioned, "al-Barbahaaree shunned seventy thousand dirhams which he inherited from his father." Ibn Abee Ya'laa said, "al-Barbahaaree strove greatly and stood firm for the Religion many times."

His Position with Regard to the People of Innovation and Deviant Sects

Imaam al-Barbahaaree, rahimahullaah, was very stern against the people of innovations and deviant sects, opposing them with his tongue and his hand, all the while following the way of Ahl us-

Sunnah wal-Jamaa'ah with regards to the treatment of the people of innovation and deviation. His desire was that this Religion remain pure and be kept free from all that the people of innovation and deviance sought to attach to it, whether the beliefs of the *Jahmiyyah*, the *Mu'tazilah*, the *Ash'arees*, the *Soofees* or the *Shee'ah* and *Raafidees*.

He makes clear the methods employed by the people of deviant sects to give sanction to their innovations and he warns us against falling into their ways and methods. He lays out for us the broad and clear outlines describing the people of deviant sects and innovations. It is as if you are looking straight at them.

In summary, his position with regard to the people of deviant sects and innovations was clearly one of opposition and sternness due to his concern and love for the *Sunnah* and due to the efforts of every deviant innovator to attack it. His position is rightfully seen as a fine example of the position of the *Imaams* of *Ahl us-Sunnah* with regard to the people of innovation, deviation and misguidance.

His Students

A large number of students learned from this *Imaam* and benefited from him since he was an example in both word and deed and from these students are:

(i) The exemplary *Imaam* and scholar, Abu 'Abdullaah ibn 'Ubaidullaah ibn Muhammad al-'Ukbaree, well-known as Ibn Battah who died in Muharram of the year 387H.[1]

(ii) The exemplary *Imaam*, well-known for his wise sayings, Muhammad ibn Ahmad ibn Isma'eel al-Baghdaadee, Abul-Husain ibn Sam'oon, the admonisher, famous for his deeds and condition. He died in the middle of Dhul-Qa'dah in the year 387H.[2]

---

1. His biography can be found in *al-'Ibr* (2/171) and *as-Siyar* (16/529).
2. His biography can be found in *al-'Ibr* (2/172) and *as-Siyar* (16/505).

(iii) Ahmad ibn Kaamil ibn Khalf ibn Shajarah, Abu Bakr. The narrator of this book from its author.

(iv) Muhammad ibn Muhammad ibn 'Uthmaan, Abu Bakr. About whom al-Khateeb (al-Baghdaadee) said, "it reaches me that he used to lead the life of an ascetic and was upon good except that he reported some things which were weak and without basis."[1]

A Glimpse of His Words and Poetry

Abu 'Abdullaah ibn Battah said: I heard Abu Muhammad al-Barbahaaree say, "Sitting in order to advise sincerely is to open the door of benefit and sitting in order to debate is to close the doors of benefit." He, *rahimahullaah*, said, "The people are in constant delusion."

From his poetry is:

"Whoever satisfies himself with what suffices him -
Begins rich and continues in following the correct way:
How fine an attribute Allaah has made being satisfied with
what suffices -
How many a humble person it has raised high
The soul of the youth feels constricted if he is poor
But if he patiently depended upon his Lord he would indeed be
given ease and sufficiency."

Trial and His Death

Imaam al-Barbahaaree, *rahimahullaah*, had renown and a position of great respect with the common people and the elite and also had status in the eyes of the ruler. However, his enemies from the people of the deviant sects and innovations did not cease in

---

1. His biography can be found in *Taarekh Baghdaad* (3/225) and *al-Meezaan* (4/28).

their efforts to incite the ruler against him and to cause anger in his heart against him, to the point that in the year 321H, the *Khaleefah* al-Qaahir ordered his minister Ibn Muqlah to arrest al-Barbahaaree and his students. Al-Barbahaaree hid, however a group of his major students were captured and taken to Basrah. Allaah, the Most High, punished Ibn Muqlah for this action by causing al-Qaahir Billaah to become angry with him, so Ibn Muqlah fled and was removed from his post and his house burned. Then al-Qaahir Billaah was himself imprisoned on the sixth of Jumaadal-Aakhirah, 322H. He was stripped of his position and blinded in both eyes. Then Allaah, the Most High, granted that al-Barbahaaree should return to his place of honour.

When Abu 'Abdullaah ibn 'Arafah, well-known as Niftawaih, died, his funeral was attended by many prominent people and scholars and the congregation was lead by al-Barbahaaree and that occurred in Safar of the year 323H. It was in this year also that al-Barbahaaree's standing grew and his words carried greater weight and his students became apparent and spread amongst the people, censuring the innovators. It reached the point that once when al-Barbahaaree was in the western side of the city, he sneezed, so his students replied to him and (were so many that) the noise they made was heard by the *Khaleefah* in his apartment, so he asked about what had happened so when he was informed he became afraid.

The innovators still did not cease trying to cause the heart of the *Khaleefah* ar-Raadee to turn against al-Barbahaaree to the point that ar-Raadee gave the order to Badr ul-Harasee, his chief of police, that he should ride out in public in Baghdaad with the proclamation that no two students of al-Barbahaaree were allowed to meet together. Again, he hid himself, having previously settled in the west of the city he now secretly moved to the east. He died in this state in the year 329H.

Ibn Abee Ya'laa said: Muhammad ibn al-Hasan al-Muqri narrated to me, saying: My grandfather and also my grandmother related to me that, "Abu Muhammad al-Barbahaaree was hidden by the sister of Toozoon in the eastern side of the town in the alleyway of the public bathhouse... he was there for about a month then his blood ceased flowing. When al-Barbahaaree died still in hiding the sister of Toozoon said to her servant, "find someone to wash him." So someone came to wash him and the door was kept locked so that no one would know. He alone stood to pray over him but when the woman who owned the house looked, she found that it was full of men wearing white and green clothing. After he had ended the (Funeral) Prayer she did not see anyone at all, so she called to her servant and said, "You have destroyed me along with my brother!" So he said, "Did you not see what I saw?", "Yes" she replied. He said, "Here are the keys to the door and it is still locked." So she said, "Bury him in my house and when I die bury me near him ..."

May Allaah have mercy upon Imaam al-Barbahaaree and grant him a great reward. He was an *Imaam* in truth, an example, knowing Allaah, and a follower of the *Sunnah*, and an unsheathed sword against the people of innovation and deviation.

Sources for his biography include:

Tabaqaatul-Hanaabilah (2/18-45), Ibn Abee Ya'laa.
Al-Muntazam (14/14-15), Ibn ul-Jawzee.
Al-Kaamil fit-Taareekh (8/378), Ibn ul-Atheer.
Al-'Ibar Fee Khabar man ghabar (2/33), adh-Dhahabee.
Siyar A'laamin-Nubalaa' (15/90-93), adh-Dhahabee.
Taareekh ul-Islaam (pp. 258-260), adh-Dhahabee.
Al-Bidaayah wan-Nihaayah (11/213-214), Ibn Katheer.
Al-Waafee bil Wafayaat (12/146-147), as-Safadee.
Al-Manhaj ul-Ahmad (2/26-39), al-'Aleemee.
Al-Maqsad ul-Arshad (1/228-230), Ibn Muflih.
Manaaqib ul-Imaam Ahmad (pp. 512-513), Ibn ul-Jawzee.

About the Book

The Title of the Book

The author did not mention any title for his book, neither in its beginning, within its texts or at its end. Perhaps, the reason for this is to be found within the matters which the author covers in his book, clarifying and explaining them and they are matters relating to the *Sunnah* i.e. *'Aqeedah* (creed) and description of its people and a warning against those in contradiction to it. So the fact that he covers these matters and briefly explains them is a clear proof that his purpose was explanation of the *Sunnah*, i.e. the *'Aqeedah* and to make them clear to the people of the *Sunnah* (*Ahl us-Sunnah*) in his time, therefore there was no further need to give a title. This along with the fact that any works written about matters of *'Aqeedah* and explanation of its details were known in the time of the author and also before his time by the name *'as-Sunnah'* just as Imaam Ahmad ibn Hanbal, *rahimahullaah*, called his book about *'Aqeedah* *'as-Sunnah.'* The same was done by his son 'Abdullaah, by al-Khallaal, al-Marwazee, al-Laalikaa'ee, Ibn Jareer and many others. Therefore those who came after him naturally identified it as *'Sharh us-Sunnah.'* Here are some of their sayings:

Ibn Abee Ya'laa said, "al-Barbahaaree wrote a number of works, from them *Sharh Kitaab is-Sunnah...*"[1]

Adh-Dhahabee said, "Abu Muhammad al-Barbahaaree wrote a number of works, from them *Sharh us-Sunnah* in which he says..."[2]

This is the name given to it by most of those who provide a biography of him.

---

1. *Tabaqaat ul-Hanaabilah* (2/18).
2. *Taarekh ul-Islaam* (the years 321-330, p.258).

The Reason for Which the Book was Written

The author did not mention in his book the reason behind compiling it. However, it is possible that there were a number of reasons which lead him to write it; perhaps the most important of these reasons are:

(i) The author's desire to convey the pure *'Aqeedah*, free from all deviations and innovations, to the people and to warn them against sitting with the people of deviation and misguidance and to explain their evils and their means of deceiving the people.

(ii) Also that innovations and deviant sects and various ideas, made alluring by Shaitaan, had become very widespread in the time of the author. So he wished to lead the people back to the correct way and the Straight Path, since he had honour in the eyes of the general public and with the elite. This point is shown by his saying: "May Allaah have mercy upon you! Examine carefully the speech of everyone you hear from in your time particularly. So do not act in haste and do not enter into anything from it until you ask and see: Did any of the Companions of the Prophet (ﷺ) speak about it or any of the scholars?"

These two reasons lead a large number of the scholars of *Ahl us-Sunnah* in his time to follow his example, as we find in the case of al-Aajurree in his book *ash-Sharee'ah* and al-Laalikaa'ee in his book *Sharh Usool I'tiqaad Ahl is-Sunnah wal-Jamaa'ah* and his student Ibn Battah in *al-Ibaanat ul-Kubraa* and *al-Ibaanat us-Sughraa* and others.

Ascription of the Book to its Author

At the beginning of the manuscript copy we find that there has been some alteration, which takes the form of the book's ascription to other than its true author. Hence, it is necessary that this be properly clarified and explained.

On the title page of the book we find: "*Kitaab Sharhis-Sunnah*, from Abu 'Abdillaah Ahmad ibn Muhammad ibn Ghaalib al-Baahilee Ghulaam Khaleel, *rahimahullaah*, the narration of Abu Bakr Ahmad ibn Kaamil ibn Khalf ibn Shajarah al-Qaadee, the narration of Abu Ishaaq Ibraaheem ibn 'Umar ibn Ahmad al-Barmakee al-Faqeeh, with permission from Abul-Hasan Muhammad ibn al-'Abbaas ibn Ahmad ibn al-Furaat, from Ibn Kaamil."

We find on the first page of the manuscript: "In the name of Allaah, the Most Merciful, the Bestower of Mercy. The Shaikh and reliable *Imaam*, Abul-Husain 'Abdul-Haqq ibn 'Abdul-Khaaliq related to us, it being read to him: Abu Taalib 'Abdul-Qaadir ibn Muhammad ibn 'Abdul-Qaadir ibn Muhammad ibn Yoosuf related to you in the congregational mosque, he listened and it was read to him: the Shaikh Abu Ishaaq Ibraaheem ibn 'Umar ibn Ahmad al-Barmakee al-Faqeeh narrated to you, amongst that which he gave permission for you to narrate from him and gave licence for, affirming that and said 'Yes'. He said: Abul-Hasan Muhammad ibn al-'Abbaas ibn Ahmad ibn al-Furaat, *rahimahullaah*, related to us from his book and it was read from his book, he said: Abu Bakr Ahmad ibn Kaamil ibn Khalf ibn Shajarah al-Qaadee narrated to us, it being read to him. He said: Abu 'Abdillaah Ahmad ibn Muhammad ibn Ghaalib al-Baahilee Ghulaam Khaleel gave this book to me and said: Narrate this book from me, from start to finish..." Then he mentioned the text of the book.

So the book was attributed to Ghulaam Khaleel and not to Abu Muhammad al-Barbahaaree. A number of observations are to be made about this:

(i) That Ghulaam Khaleel was a liar and a fabricator. Here are some of the sayings of the scholars about him:

Ad-Daarqutnee said, "Abandoned (*matrook*)."[1]

---

1. *Ad-Du'afaa' wal-Matrookeen* (p.122) and *al-Majrooheen* (1/150).

Ibn at-Tammaar al-Warraaq reports: Abu Daawood as-Sijjistaanee did not openly declare anyone a liar except two men: al-Kadeemee and Ghulaam Khaleel. He said about the last of the two, "I fear that he is the Dajjaal of Baghdaad. He has presented his *ahaadeeth* before me, so I examined four hundred *ahaadeeth* and found that all their chains of narrations and texts were lies."[1]

Ibn 'Adiyy said, "I heard Abu 'Abdillaah an-Nahawandee saying: I said to Ghulaam Khaleel 'What are these heart melting narrations that you narrate?' He said 'We fabricate them so that the hearts of the common people should become tender.'"[2]

Al-Haakim said: I heard the Shaikh Abu Bakr ibn Ishaaq saying, "Ahmad ibn Muhammad ibn Ghaalib is one of those whose being a liar I do not doubt."[3]

Adh-Dhahabee said, "Ghulaam Khaleel is well-known for fabricating *ahaadeeth*."[4]

Refer to the biography of Ghulaam Khaleel in *Meezaanul-I'tidaal* (1/141) and *as-Siyar* (13/283).

(ii) Ghulaam Khaleel died in the month of Rajab in the year 275H. However, we find in the book, point number 112: "Everything that I have described to you in this book, it is from Allaah, the Most High, from the Messenger of Allaah (ﷺ), from his Companions, from the *Taabi'een* and from the third generation to the fourth." This shows that the book was not written by him, since he died in the last quarter of the third century and did not reach the fourth century at all. Whereas, al-Barbahaaree died in the year 329H, so he reached the fourth century and therefore mentioned it.

(iii) That Ibn Kaamil, the narrator of this book, did perhaps narrate from Ghulaam Khaleel but at a very young age, since he was born in the year 260H, i.e. fifteen years before the death of

---

1. *Taareekh Baghdaad* (5/79).
2. *Al-Kaamil* (1/198) of Ibn 'Adiyy.
3. *Lisaanul-Meezaan* (1/273).
4. *Al-Mughnee fid-Du'afaa'* (1/57).

Ghulaam Khaleel. However, it is more likely and proper that he narrated from Abu Muhammad al-Barbahaaree, since he lived along with him for a long period of time, since Ibn Kaamil died in the year 350H and as has preceded al-Barbahaaree died in the year 329H. So perhaps the persecution of al-Barbahaaree and his students by the ruler lead to some of the scribes to change the name of the author for fear that they would be seized and punished if they were found to have any connection with al-Barbahaaree; Allaah knows best. Ibn Kaamil was one of the great preservers of knowledge and author of various works. His biography can be found in *al-'Ibar* (2/83) and *as-Siyar* (15/544).

(iv) That most of those who provide a biography of al-Barbahaaree state that he wrote a book entitled *Sharhus-Sunnah*, whereas, we do not find any mention of its like in the biographies of Ghulaam Khaleel.

A number of the scholars came across this book and quoted from it and benefited from it agreeing to its ascription to Imaam al-Barbahaaree, as is seen by what follows:

(i) Ibn Abee Ya'laa in *Tabaqaat ul-Hanaabilah* (2/18-43) quotes the whole text of the book except for a very small number of lines and quotes everything found in the manuscript except for the first two sheets and he says before it, "al-Barbahaaree wrote a number of works, from them *Sharh Kitaab is-Sunnah* in which he mentioned: Beware of smaller innovations..." to the end of the book.

(ii) Shaikh ul-Islaam Ibn Taimiyyah quotes from it in his book *Bughyat ul-Murtaad* (p.258), saying, "It is reported from Abu Muhammad al-Barbahaaree that he said: Intellect is not acquired, rather it is a blessing from Allaah." This text is to be found in the book as point number 77.

(iii) Adh-Dhahabee also quotes from it in *al-'Uluww* (p.244 of the abridged version) quoting from point number 13 and what follows it.

(iv) A large section or a portion is quoted, in the same way as Ibn Abee Ya'laa, by Abul-Yaman al-'Aleemee in *al-Manhaj ul-Ahmad* (2/27-37) and by Ibn ul-'Imaad al-Hanbalee in *ash-Shudharaat* (2/319-322) and by adh-Dhahabee in *Taarekh ul-Islaam* (Events and deaths in the years 321-330H p.258) and by him in *Siyar A'laamin-Nubalaa'* (15/91).

In conclusion these are definite proofs of the correctness of the ascription of the book to Imaam al-Barbahaaree. All praise and thanks are for Allaah.

Manuscripts of the Book

There is a photocopy of the manuscript in the main library of Ummul-Quraa University, Makkah, bearing the collection number thirteen. It is written in legible writing and was written in the year 506H, or just after. This manuscript is the one having the chain of narration from Ghulaam Khaleel written upon it. It has an average of fifteen lines per page.[1]

As regards the other copy, it is that which has been printed within *Tabaqaatul-Hanaabilah* (vol.2, pp.18-45) of Ibn Abee Ya'laa.

---

1. Appendix 1 (pp. 110-112) shows the title page, the first page and the last page of this manuscript.

بِسْمِ اللَّهِ الرَّحْمَنِ الرَّحِيمِ

The Text of the Book

All praise is for Allaah who guided us to Islaam and blessed us with it and placed us in the best nation, so we ask Him to grant us that we keep to that which He loves and is pleased with and avoid that which He hates and which angers Him.

1 Know that Islaam is the *Sunnah* and the *Sunnah* is Islaam[1] and one of them cannot be established without the other.

---

1. The Prophet (ﷺ) said, *"He who turns away from my Sunnah is not from me."* Reported by al-Bukhaaree (Eng. trans. 7/1-2/no.1), Muslim (Eng. trans. 2/703/no.3236) and an-Nasaa'ee.

Abu Hurairah said that Allaah's Messenger (ﷺ) said, *"All of my Ummah will enter Paradise except those who refuse."* It was said, *"Who will refuse?"* He replied, *"Whoever obeys me enters Paradise and whoever disobeys me has refused."* Reported by al-Bukhaaree (Eng. trans. 9/284/no.384).

Imaam az-Zuhree (the famous *taabi'ee*, d.124H) said, "The people of knowledge who came before us used to say, 'Salvation lies in clinging to the *Sunnah*.'" Reported by ad-Daarimee in his *Sunan* (no.96).

Imaam Maalik said, "The *Sunnah* is like the Ark of Noah. Whoever embarks upon it reaches salvation and whoever refuses is drowned." Quoted by Shaikh ul-Islaam Ibn Taimiyyah in *Majmoo' ul-Fataawaa* (4/57).

23

2   From the *Sunnah* is clinging to the *Jamaa'ah*.[1] Whoever desires other than the *Jamaa'ah* and departs from it then he has thrown off the yoke of Islaam from his neck and he is astray, leading others astray.[2]

3   The foundation upon which the *Jamaa'ah* is built is the Companions of Muhammad (ﷺ). May Allaah's Mercy be upon them all. They are *Ahl us-Sunnah wal-Jamaa'ah*,[3] so whoever does

---

1. 'Umar, *radiallaahu 'anhu,* reports that the Prophet (ﷺ) said, *"Stick to the Jamaa'ah and beware of splitting for Shaitaan is found along with the single person but is further from two. Whoever desires the centre of Paradise then let him stick to the Jamaa'ah. He whose good deed pleases him and his evil deed causes him to feel bad then he is a believer."* Reported by Ahmad (1/18), at-Tirmidhee (no. 2165) and al-Haakim (1/114) and is declared *saheeh* by Shaikh al-Albaanee in *as-Saheehah* (no. 1116).

Anas, *radiallaahu 'anhu,* reports that the Prophet (ﷺ) said, *"Indeed the Children of Israa'eel divided into seventy one sects and my Ummah will divide into seventy two sects, all of them in the fire except one and that is the Jamaa'ah."* Reported by Ibn Maajah (no. 3993) and declared *saheeh* by Shaikh al-Albaanee.

2. Alluding to the *hadeeth* of Ibn 'Abbaas, *radiallaahu 'anhummaa,* who said: Allaah's Messenger (ﷺ) said, *"He who sees from his ruler something he dislikes, let him be patient with him, for he who splits away from the Jamaa'ah by a handspan and then dies, dies a death of Jaahiliyyah"* and in a narration, *"then he has thrown off the yoke of Islaam from his neck."* Reported by al-Bukhaaree (Eng. trans. 9/145), Muslim and Ahmad and the other narration by at-Tirmidhee (no. 2867) and Ahmad (4/130). Refer to *Sharh ul-'Aqeedut-Tahaawiyyah* (pp. 379-382), checked by Shaikh Naasir ud-Deen al-Albaanee.

3. As is shown by the *hadeeth* of at-Tirmidhee (no. 2641): 'Abdullaah ibn 'Amr said: The Messenger of Allaah (ﷺ) said, *"What happened to the Children of Israa'eel will happen with my Ummah, just as one shoe resembles the other, to the point that if one of them had intercourse with his mother openly, there would be someone who did that in my Ummah. The Children of Israa'eel split into seventy two sects and my Ummah will split into seventy three sects, all of which are in the Fire except one sect."* They asked, "Which is that one, O Messenger of Allaah?" He replied, *"That which I and my Companions are upon."* Declared *hasan* by Shaikh al-Albaanee.   =

24

not take from them has gone astray and innovated[1] and every innovation is misguidance, and misguidance and its people are in the Fire.[2]

4   'Umar ibn al-Khattaab, *rahimahullaah,* said, "There is no excuse for anyone going astray thinking that he is upon guidance. Nor for abandoning guidance thinking it to be misguidance, since the affairs have been made clear, the proof established[3] and the excuse cut off."[4] That is because the *Sunnah* and the *Jamaa'ah* have

---

Abu Shaamah (d.665H) said, "The order to stick to the *Jamaa'ah* means sticking to the truth and its followers; even if those who stick to the truth are few and those who oppose it are many, since the truth is that which the first *Jamaa'ah* from the time of the Prophet (صلى الله عليه وسلم) and his Companions, *radiallaahu 'anhum,* were upon. No attention is given to the great number of the people of futility coming after them." (*Al-Baa'ith 'alal-Bida'h wal-Hawaadith,* p.19).

1. It is authentically reported that Allaah's Messenger (صلى الله عليه وسلم) said, "*Stick to my Sunnah and the Sunnah of the rightly-guided Caliphs after me, cling to that with your molar teeth and beware of new matters, for every innovation is misguidance.*" Reported by Ahmad, Abu Daawood (Eng. trans. 3/1294/no.4590), at-Tirmidhee (no. 2676), Ibn Maajah (no. 42), ad-Daarimee (no. 96) and Ibn Abee 'Aasim in *as-Sunnah* (no. 54). Shaikh al-Albaanee declares, "Its *isnaad* is *saheeh,* its narrators reliable."

2. Jaabir, *radiallaahu 'anhu,* reports that the Prophet (صلى الله عليه وسلم) would say in his *khutbah,* "*... The most truthful speech is the Book of Allaah. The best way is the way of Muhammad. The worst of affairs are the novelties and every novelty is an innovation and every innovation is misguidance and every misguidance is in the Fire.*" Reported by an-Nasaa'ee (3/188). It is declared *saheeh* by Shaikh al-Albaanee in *Saheeh Sunan in-Nasaa'ee* (no. 1487).

3. Al-'Irbaad ibn Saariyah, *radiallaahu 'anhu,* reports that the Prophet (صلى الله عليه وسلم) said, "*.... I have left you upon clear guidance. Its night is like its day. No one deviates from it after me except that he is destroyed.*" Reported by Ahmad, Ibn Maajah (no. 43) and al-Haakim. It is declared *saheeh* by Shaikh al-Albaanee in *as-Saheehah* (no. 937).

4. Reported by Ibn Battah in *al-Ibaantul-Kubraa* (no. 162) by way of al-Awzaa'ee that it reached him that 'Umar ibn al-Khattaab said it. However, its chain is *munqati'* (disconnected).

Al-Marwazee reports in *as-Sunnah* (no. 95) that 'Umar ibn 'Abd al-'Azeez said, "There is no excuse for anyone, after the *Sunnah,* to be misguided upon error which he thought was guidance."

25

consolidated and safeguarded all of the Religion. It has been made clear to the people, so it is upon the people to comply and follow.[1]

5 May Allaah have mercy upon you. Know that the Religion is what came from Allaah, the Blessed and Most High. It is not something left to the intellect and opinions of men. Knowledge of it is what comes from Allaah and His Messenger (ﷺ), so do not follow anything based upon your desires and so deviate away from the Religion and leave Islaam. There will be no excuse for you since Allaah's Messenger (ﷺ) explained the *Sunnah* to his *Ummah* and made it clear to his Companions and they are the *Jamaa'ah*, and they are the Main Body (*as-Sawaad ul-A'dham*), and the Main Body is the truth and its followers.[2]

---

1. 'Abdullaah ibn Mas'ood, *radiallaahu 'anhu*, said, "Follow and do not innovate, for you have been given that which is sufficient and every innovation is misguidance." Reported by Abu Khaithamah in *Kitaab ul-'Ilm* (no. 540) and declared *saheeh* by Shaikh al-Albaanee.

2. Imaam Ahmad reports in his *musnad* (4/278) with *hasan isnaad* the narration of Nu'maan ibn Basheer: Abu Umaamah al-Baahilee, *radiallaahu 'anhu,* said, "Stick to the main body (*as-Sawaadul - a'dham*), so a man said, "What is the 'Main Body'? So Abu Umaamah said, "This *Aayah* (54) in Soorah an-Noor:

$$\text{فَإِن تَوَلَّوۡاْ فَإِنَّمَا عَلَيۡهِ مَا حُمِّلَ وَعَلَيۡكُم مَّا حُمِّلۡتُمۡ}$$

But if you turn away, he (Muhammad ﷺ) is only responsible for the duty placed on him and you for that placed on you."

Ibn Mas'ood, *radiallaahu 'anhu,* said, "The *Jamaa'ah* is what conforms to the truth, even if you are alone." Reported by Ibn 'Asaakir in *Taareekh Dimashq* with a *saheeh isnaad* as pointed out by Shaikh al-Albaanee in *al-Mishkaat* (1/61).

So he who contradicts the Companions of Allaah's Messenger (صلى الله عليه وسلم) in any of the affairs of the Religion then he has fallen into disbelief.[1]

6 Know that people never introduce an innovation until they abandon its like from the *Sunnah*.[2] So, beware of newly invented matters, since every newly invented matter is an innovation and every innovation is misguidance and misguidance and its people are in the Fire.

---

1. Allaah, the Most High, did not only warn against opposing His Messenger (صلى الله عليه وسلم) but also warned against the following of any way other than that of the first Believers: the Companions, *radiallaahu 'anhum,* amongst whom the Qur'aan was sent down and who learned directly from the Messenger (صلى الله عليه وسلم). Allaah, the Most High says:

$$وَمَن يُشَاقِقِ ٱلرَّسُولَ مِنۢ بَعْدِ مَا تَبَيَّنَ لَهُ ٱلْهُدَىٰ وَيَتَّبِعْ غَيْرَ سَبِيلِ ٱلْمُؤْمِنِينَ نُوَلِّهِۦ مَا تَوَلَّىٰ وَنُصْلِهِۦ جَهَنَّمَ ۖ وَسَآءَتْ مَصِيرًا ﴿١١٥﴾$$

If anyone contends with the Messenger even after guidance has been plainly conveyed to him and follows a path other than that of the Believers (i.e. the Companions), We shall leave him in the path he has chosen and land him in Hell. What an evil refuge!

Soorah an-Nisaa' (4):115

So he who totally abandons their way and instead follows the way of the devils, like the extreme *Raafidess, Baatinees* and the extreme *Soofees* who worship others besides Allaah, then he has left the Religion.

2. Hassan ibn 'Atiyyah, *rahimahullaah,* said, "A people never introduce an innovation into their Religion except that Allaah takes away its like from their *Sunnah* and then does not restore it to them until the Day of Resurrection." Reported by ad-Daarimee and declared *saheeh* by Shaikh al-Albaanee in *al-Mishkaat* (1/66/no.188).

27

7 Beware of small innovations because they grow until they become large.[1]

---

1. A striking example of how small innovations lead a person into committing major innovations is found in the narration reported by ad-Daarimee in his *Sunan* (1/79):

'Amr ibn Salmah said: We used to sit by the door of 'Abdullaah ibn Mas'ood before the Morning Prayer, so that when he came out we would walk with him to the mosque. (One day) Abu Moosaa al-Ash'aree came to us and said, "Has Abu 'Abd ar-Rahmaan come out yet?" We replied, "No." So he sat down with us until he came out. When he came out we all stood along with him, so Abu Moosaa said to him, "O Abu 'Abd ar-Rahmaan! I have just seen something in the mosque which I deemed to be evil, but all praise is for Allaah, I did not see anything except good." He enquired, "Then what is it?" (Abu Moosaa) replied, "If you live you will see it. I saw in the mosque people sitting in circles awaiting the Prayer. In each circle they had pebbles in their hands and a man would say 'repeat *Allaahu Akbar* a hundred times.' So they would repeat it a hundred times. Then he would say, 'say *Laa ilaaha illallaah* a hundred times.' So they would say it a hundred times. Then he would say, 'say *Subhaanallaah* a hundred times.' So they would say it a hundred times." (Ibn Mas'ood) asked, "What did you say to them?" (Abu Moosaa) said, "I did not say anything to them. Instead I waited to hear your view or what you declared." (Ibn Mas'ood) replied, "Would that you had ordered them to count up the evil deeds they acquired and assured them that their good deeds would not be lost!" Then we went along with him (Ibn Mas'ood) until he came to one of these circles and stood and said, "What is this which I see you doing?" They replied, "O Abu 'Abd ar-Rahmaan! These are pebbles upon which we are counting *takbeer*, *tahleel* and *tasbeeh*." He said, "Count up your evil deeds. I assure you that none of your good deeds will be lost. Woe to you, O *Ummah* of Muhammad (ﷺ)! How quickly you go to destruction! These are the Companions of your Prophet (ﷺ) and who are widespread. There is his (ﷺ) clothes which have not yet decayed and his bowl which is unbroken. By Him in Whose Hand is my soul! Either you are upon a Religion better guided than the Religion of Muhammad (ﷺ) or that you are opening the door of misguidance." They said, "O Abu 'Abd ar-Rahmaan! By Allaah, we only intended good." He said, "How many there are who intend good but do not achieve it. Indeed Allaah's Messenger (ﷺ) said to us 'A people will recite the Qur'aan but it will not pass beyond their throats.' By Allaah! I do not know, perhaps most of them are from you." Then he left them.

Umar ibn Salmah (the sub-narrator) said: We saw most of those people fighting against us on the day of Nahrawaan, along with the *Khawaarij*.

Authenticated by Saleem al-Hilaalee in *al-Bid'ah* (pp. 26-29).

This was the case with every innovation introduced in this *Ummah*. It began as something small, bearing resemblance to the truth which is why those who entered it were mislead and then were unable to leave it. So it grew and became the religion which they followed and thus deviated from the Straight Path and left Islaam.[1]

8 May Allaah have mercy upon you! Examine carefully the speech of everyone you hear from in your time particularly. So do not act in haste and do not enter into anything from it until you ask and see: Did any of the Companions of the Prophet (ﷺ) speak about it or any of the scholars? So if you find a narration from them about it, cling to it, do not go beyond it for anything[2] and do not give precedence to anything over it and thus fall into the Fire.

9 Know that leaving the correct path occurs in two ways. Firstly: that a man strays from the correct path intending nothing but good, so his error is not to be followed since it leads to destruction. (Secondly), a man who deliberately opposes the truth and acts contrary to the Pious ones who came before him, he is astray, leading others astray, a rebellious devil within the *Ummah*. It is a duty upon those who know of him to warn the people against him and to explain his condition to them so that no one falls into his innovation and is destroyed.

---

1. The scholars differentiate between those innovations which take a person outside the fold of Islaam (*al-Bid'atul - Mukaffirah*) and those which do not. So this is not to be understood unrestrictedly.

2. Imaam al-Awzaa'ee, *rahimahullaah*, said, "Knowledge is what comes from the Companions of Muhammad (ﷺ) and that which does not come from a single one of them is not knowledge". Refer to *Jaami 'Bayaanil- 'Ilm* of Ibn 'Abdul Barr (2/36).

10 May Allaah have mercy upon you! Know that a servant's Islaam is not complete until he follows, attests to and submits to (the truth). So anyone who claims that there remains anything from Islaam not sufficiently explained by the Companions of Allaah's Messenger (ﷺ), has falsely accused them, has split from them and spoken ill of them. He is an innovator, astray and leading others astray, introducing into Islaam that which is not from it.[1]

11 May Allaah have mercy upon you! Know that the *Sunnah* is not a matter for analogies or reasoning with examples and desires are not to be followed in it. Rather, it is just a case of affirming the narrations from Allaah's Messenger (ﷺ), without asking how, explaining or saying: 'Why?' or 'How?'

---

1. Ibn Mas'ood, *radiallaahu 'anhu*, described the Companions of the Messenger of Allaah (ﷺ) saying, "Allaah looked into the hearts of the servants and found the heart of Muhammad to be the best of hearts, so He chose him for Himself and sent with him His Revelation, then He looked into the hearts of the servants after the heart of Muhammad (ﷺ) and found the hearts of his Companions to be the best of the hearts of the servants, so He made them the helpers of His Prophet, fighting for His Religion. So that which the Muslims hold to be good is good with Allaah and that which they hold to be bad is bad with Allaah." Reported in the *Musnad* of Imaam Ahmad (1/379) and declared *hasan* by Shaikh al-Albaanee in *ad-Da'eefah* (2/17).

12 Debating, arguing and disputing are innovations which throw doubt into the heart, even if the person reaches the truth and the *Sunnah*.[1]

13 May Allaah have mercy upon you! Know that speculative speech about the Lord, the Most High, is a newly invented matter and is an innovation and misguidance. Nothing is to be said about the Lord except what He, the Mighty and Majestic, described Himself with in the Qur'aan and what the Messenger of Allaah (ﷺ) explained to his Companions. So, He, the Majestic, is One:

---

1. Allaah, the Most High, says:

مَا يُجَٰدِلُ فِىٓ ءَايَٰتِ ٱللَّهِ إِلَّا ٱلَّذِينَ كَفَرُواْ

None dispute about the signs of Allaah, except those who disbelieve.

Soorah Ghaafir (40):4

At-Tirmidhee reports a *hasan hadeeth* from Abu Umaamah, who said: Allaah's Messenger (ﷺ) said, *"A people never went astray after being upon guidance except through disputation."* Then Allaah's Messenger (ﷺ) recited this *Aayah*:

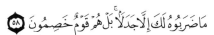

مَا ضَرَبُوهُ لَكَ إِلَّا جَدَلًۢا بَلْ هُمْ قَوْمٌ خَصِمُونَ ٥٨

This they set forth to you, only by way of argument. Nay, but they are a contentious people.

Soorah az-Zukhruf (43):58

Al-Aajurree reports in *ash-Sharee'ah* (p.57) that a man came to al-Hasan (al-Basree) and said, "O Abu Sa'eed! Let me debate with you about the Religion." Al-Hasan replied, "As for me, I know my Religion. If you have lost your Religion then go and look for it."

'Umar ibn 'Abdul-'Azeez, *rahimahullaah,* said, "He who allows his Religion to be open to disputing will frequently change over." See *Jaami' Bayaanil 'Ilm* (2/113).

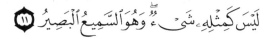

There is nothing like Him and He is the All-Hearing, the All-Seeing.[1]

14 Our Lord is the First without any 'when' and the Last without any end. He knows what is secret and what is more hidden. He ascended over His *'Arsh* (Throne) and His knowledge is in every place and no place is free of His knowledge.[2]

15 No one says about the attributes of the Lord, the Most High, 'Why?' except one who doubts about Allaah, the Blessed and Most High. The Qur'aan is the Speech of Allaah, His Revelation and Light. It is not created, since the Qur'aan is from Allaah and that which is from Allaah is not created. This was what Maalik ibn Anas, Ahmad ibn Hanbal and the scholars before and after them said and debating about it is disbelief.[3]

---

1. Soorah ash-Shoora (42):11

2. Many *Aayaat* of the Qur'aan and *ahaadeeth* of the Prophet (ﷺ) affirm that Allaah is above His Throne. Numerous sayings have been reported from the Pious Predecessors emphasising this important belief. See appendix 2 (pp. 113-115).

3. The Qur'aan is the Speech of Allaah, hence it is an attribute of Allaah. All of Allaah's attributes have been with Him eternally.

Imaam Maalik said, "The Qur'aan is the speech of Allaah. It is not created." Reported by al-Laalikaa'ee in *Sharh Usool I'tiqaad Ahl is-Sunnah* (no.414).

Imaam Ahmad ibn Hanbal was asked about one who says that the Qur'aan is created, so he said, "(He is) a disbeliever." Reported by al-Laalikaa'ee in *Sharh Usool I'tiqaad Ahl is-Sunnah* (no.449).

16 To have Faith in seeing Allaah on the Day of Resurrection. They will see Allaah with the eyes of their heads.[1] He will take account of them without anyone acting on His behalf or any interpreter.[2]

---

1. Allaah says:

Some faces that Day shall be shining and radiant. Looking at their Lord.

Soorah al-Qiyaamah (75):22-23

Suhaib reports that Allaah's Messenger (ﷺ) said, *"When the people of Paradise enter Paradise, Allaah, the Blessed and Most High, will say 'Do you wish for anything extra that I may give you?' They will say 'Have you not brightened our faces? Have You not entered us into Paradise and saved us from the Fire?' So He will remove the screen and they will not have been given anything as beloved to them as looking at their Lord, the Mighty and Majestic."* Reported by Muslim (Eng. trans. 1/114/no.347) and others.

Hanbal said: I spoke to Abu 'Abdullaah, meaning Ahmad (ibn Hanbal) about seeing Allaah (*ar-Ru'yah*). He said, "They are authentic *ahaadeeth*. We have Faith (*Eemaan*) in them and affirm it. We have Faith in and affirm everything reported from the Prophet (ﷺ) with good chains of narration." Reported by al-Laalikaa'ee in *Sharh Usool I'tiqaad Ahl is-Sunnah* (no.889).

2. 'Adiyy ibn Haatim reports that the Prophet (ﷺ) said, *"There is not one of you except that Allaah will speak to him on the Day of Resurrection, there being no interpreter between Him and him."* Reported by al-Bukhaaree (Eng. trans. 8/358/no.547), Ahmad and at-Tirmidhee.

17 To believe in the Balance (*Meezaan*) on the Day of Resurrection, upon which good and evil will be weighed. It has two scales and a tongue.[1]

---

1. Allaah, the Most High, says:

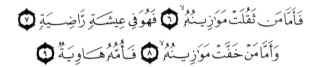

As for him whose balance (of good deeds) will be heavy, he will live a pleasant life (in Paradise). But, as for him whose balance (of good deeds) will be light, he will have his home in a pit (i.e. Hell).

Soorah al-Qaari'ah (101):6-7

Abu Hurairah, *radiallaahu 'anhu,* reports that Allaah's Messenger (ﷺ) said, *"Two words are most beloved to the Most Merciful, light upon the tongue and heavy upon the Balance: Subhaanallaahi wa bihamdihi and Subhaanallaahil 'Adheem."* *Reported* by al-Bukhaaree (Eng. trans. 9/489-490/no.652).

The *'Hadeeth* of the Parchment': 'Abdullaah ibn 'Amr ibn al 'Aas said: I heard Allaah's Messenger (ﷺ) say, *"Allaah will take out a man from my Ummah before the creation on the Day of Resurrection and ninety-nine scrolls will be unrolled for him. Each one as long as the eye can see. Then He will say 'Do you deny any of this? Have my watchful scribes wronged you?' He will reply 'No, O my Lord!' So, He (Allaah) will say 'Do you have any excuse (or any good deed)? So he will reply 'No, O my Lord!' So, He (Allaah) will say 'Rather you do possess a good deed with Us and you will not be wronged this Day.' So a parchment is brought containing 'I bear witness that none has the right to be worshipped except Allaah and I bear witness that Muhammad is His slave and Messenger.' So He (Allaah) will say 'Witness the weighing.' So he will reply 'O my Lord! What is this parchment compared to those great scrolls?' So He (Allaah) will say 'Indeed you will not be wronged.' So the scrolls will be placed on one scale and the parchment on the other scale. So the scrolls will be lighter and the parchment heavier. Nothing will outweigh the name of Allaah."* *Reported* by Ahmad, at-Tirmidhee and Ibn Maajah. Shaikh al-Albaanee declared it *saheeh* in *Saheeh Sunan at-Tirmidhee.*

18 To have Faith in the punishment of the grave and Munkar and Nakeer.[1]

---

1. To have Faith (*Eemaan*) in the punishment of the grave has the consensus (*ijmaa'*) of *Ahl us-Sunnah wal-Jamaa'ah*, as has been declared by Abul-Hasan al-Ash'aree (*Risaalah ilaa Ahlilth-Thaghr*, p.279), being denied only by the *Khawaarij* and some of the *Mu'tazilah*.

Allaah, the Most High, says:

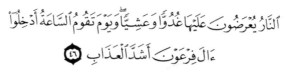

In front of the Fire will they be brought morning and evening and on the Day when the Hour will established (it will be said to the angels): Cause Pharaoh's people to enter the severest torment!

Soorah Ghaafir (40):46

Ibn 'Abbaas said: Allaah's Messenger (ﷺ) passed by two graves and said, "*Indeed they are being punished but they are not being punished for something major.*" Then he said, "*Rather it is so: one of them did not used to protect himself from being soiled with his urine. The other used to go about telling stories (to cause enmity)...*" Reported by al-Bukhaaree (Eng. trans. 1/141/no.215), Muslim (Eng. trans. 1/171/no.575), Ahmad and the compilers of the four *Sunan*.

Abu Hurairah reports that Allaah's Messenger (ﷺ) said, "*When the deceased (or 'one of you') is put in the grave, two black angels having blue eyes come to him. One of them is called al-Munkar and the other an-Nakeer and they will say.....*" Reported by at-Tirmidhee and declared *hasan* by Shaikh al-Albaanee in *Saheeh al-Jaami'*.

There are many *ahaadeeth* concerning the punishment of the grave. Al-Baihaqee wrote a whole treatise entitled *Ithbaat 'Adhaab al-Qabr*, consisting of some 240 narrations.

Imaam ash-Shaafi'ee (d.204H) said, "The punishment of the grave is true, the questioning of those in the graves is true, the Resurrection is true, the Day of Judgement is true, Paradise and the Fire are true. Whatever else is reported in the *Sunnah* and so mentioned by the scholars and their follower throughout the lands of the Muslims is true." Reported by al-Baihaqee *Manaaqib ash-Shaafi'ee* (1/415).

19 To have Faith in the Pool (*Hawd*) of Allah's Messenger (ﷺ). Every Prophet has a Pool, except for Saalih, *'alaihis-Salaam*, because his Pool was the udder of his she-camel.[1]

Imaam Ahmad ibn Hanbal (d.241H) said, "The principles of the *Sunnah* with us are: To cling to that which the Companions of Allaah's Messenger (ﷺ) were upon and to follow them .... to have Faith in the punishment of the grave and that this *Ummah* will be tested in their graves and asked about Faith and Islaam, who his Lord is and who his Prophet is. Munkar and Nakeer will come to him as Allaah wills and however Allaah wishes." From *Usool us-Sunnah* of Imaam Ahmad.

Imaam Ahmad said, "Punishment of the grave is true. No one denies it except one who is misguided and astray and leading others astray." Reported by Ibn Abee Ya'laa in *Tabaqaat ul-Hanaabilah* (1/174).

1. The explainer of *at-Tahaawiyyah* said, "The *ahaadeeth* reported about the Pool reach the level of *mutawaatir*, being reported by more than 30 Companions."

Anas ibn Maalik, *radiallaahu 'anhu*, reports that Allaah's Messenger (ﷺ) said, *"The size of my Pool is like what is between Jerusalem and San'aa in Yemen and it has drinking cups like the number of stars in the sky."* Reported by al-Bukhaaree (Eng. trans. 8/380/no.582), Ahmad and at-Tirmidhee.

Samurah reports that Allaah's Messenger (ﷺ) said, *"There will be a Pool for every Prophet. They will vie with regards to who has the greater number of people coming to it. I hope from Allaah that I will have the greater number."* Reported by at-Tirmidhee and others. Shaikh al-Albaanee declared it *saheeh* in *as-Saheehah* (no. 1589).

As regards the exception quoted for Saalih, *'alaihis-salaam*, the narrations about that are not authentic.

36

20 To have Faith in the Intercession (*Shafaa'ah*) of Allaah's Messenger (ﷺ) on the Day of Resurrection for those guilty of sins, those upon the bridge and to cause them to come out from within the Fire. There is intercession for every Prophet. Likewise for their eminently truthful and sincere followers, the martyrs and the pious. After that Allaah bestows His grace abundantly upon those whom He pleases and people are taken out of the Fire after having been burnt and reduced to charcoal.[1]

---

1. The long *hadeeth* of the Intercession is reported by al-Bukhaaree (Eng. trans. vol. 6 no. 236) and Muslim (Eng. trans. vol. 1, pp. 122-135).

Concerning the types of intercession, Shaikh 'Abdul-'Azeez ibn Baaz, *haafidhahullaah*, says in his notes on *al-'Aqeedah al-Waasitiyyah* (p.73), "The different intercessions that will occur on the Day of Resurrection are six and are well-known from the *Sharee'ah* proofs. From them, three are particular to the Prophet (ﷺ). The six types are:

(i) The Major Intercession, which is for judgement to commence for those gathered for it. (ii) Intercession for the people of Paradise to enter it. (iii) His (ﷺ) intercession for the punishment to be lightened for his uncle Abu Taalib, so that he is placed in a shallow part of Hell-Fire. This form of intercession is particular to the Prophet (ﷺ) for his uncle Abu Taalib. As for other disbelievers, there is no intercession for them. He, the Most High, said:

So no intercession of intercessors will be of any use to them.

Soorah al-Mudathir (74):48

(iv) Intercession for some of those who deserve the Fire not to enter it. (v) Intercession for those who enter the Fire to come out of it. (vi) His Intercession for the raising of the ranks of the people of Paradise. This last intercession is general for the Prophet (ﷺ) and other Prophets, the righteous, the angels and for Muslim children who died whilst they were young.

All of these are only for the people who were upon *Tawheed*. As regards the sinful from the people of *Tawheed* who enter it (the Fire), they will not remain in it but will be brought out after being purified. It is established in the *Saheeh* from the Prophet (ﷺ) that the sinful will die in it, then will be brought out like charcoal. Then, they will sprout (in Paradise) like shoots upon a riverbank."

21 To have Faith in the Bridge over Hell. The Bridge seizes whomever Allaah pleases, allows passage to whomever Allaah pleases and causes whomever Allaah pleases to fall into Hell. The people are preceded by light according to their level of Faith.[1]

22 To have Faith in the Prophets and Angels.[2]

---

1. Allaah, the Most High, says:

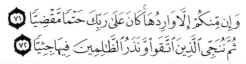

There is not one of you but will pass over it (Hell); this is, with your Lord, a decree which must be accomplished. But We shall save those who used to fear Allaah and were dutiful to Him and We shall leave the wrongdoers therein, (humbled) to their knees.

Soorah Maryam (19):71-72

There occurs in a long *hadeeth* reported by Abu Sa'eed al-Khudree in *Saheeh Muslim* (Eng. trans. vol.1, no.352) that the Prophet (ﷺ) said, *"....Then the bridge will be laid over Hell-Fire and intercession allowed and they will say 'O Allaah! Grant us safety, grant us safety.'"* It was said, "O Messenger of Allaah! What is the bridge?" He replied, *"That which is extremely slippery. Upon it are hooks, claws and barbs like the thorns of Najd called as-Sa'daan. So the believers will pass like the blink of an eye, like the lightening, like the wind, like the birds and like fast horses and camels. Some will be saved, some will be lacerated then set free and some will be thrown into the Fire...."*

2. Allaah, the Most High, says:

The Messenger believes in what has been revealed to Him from his Lord, as do the believers. Each one (of them) believes in Allaah, His Angels, His Books and His Messengers. (They say): We make no distinction between one and another of His Messengers.

Soorah al-Baqarah (2):285

23 To have Faith that Paradise is true and real and that the Fire is true and real and that both are already created.[1] Paradise is in the seventh Heaven. Its ceiling is the Throne. The Fire is beneath the seventh and lowest earth. They are both created. Allaah, the Most High, knew the number of inhabitants of Paradise and those who would enter it and the number of those who are the inhabitants of the Fire and those who would enter it. Neither of them will ever end; they will both last along with Allaah for ever and ever.

24 Aadam, *'alaihis-salaam*, was present in the everlasting and created Paradise but was removed from it after disobeying Allaah, the Mighty and Majestic.

25 To have Faith in al-Maseehud-Dajjaal.[2]

26 To have Faith in the descent of 'Eesaa, the son of Maryam, *'alaihis-salaam*. He will descend, kill Dajjaal, marry, and pray behind the leader of the Muslims who is from the family of Muhammad (ﷺ) and he will die and be buried by the Muslims.[3]

---

1. The *hadeeth* of the *Israa* and *Mi'raaj* shows the present existence of Paradise and the Fire. It occurs in *Saheeh al-Bukhaaree* (Eng. trans. vol.5, no.227) and *Saheeh Muslim* (Eng. trans. vol.1, no.s 309-322). *Raf'ul-Astaar* by al-Ameer as-San'aanee is an excellent book being a reply to those who claim that the Fire will eventually come to an end.

2. From the many *ahaadeeth* about the Dajjaal is what al-Bukhaaree reports in his *Saheeh* (Eng. trans. vol.9, no.245) from Anas, *radiallaahu 'anhu,* that the Prophet (ﷺ) said, *"No Prophet was sent except that he warned his nation about the one-eyed liar (i.e. Dajjaal). Beware! He is blind in one eye, whereas your Lord is not so. There will be written between his (Dajjaal's) eyes: Kaafir."*

3. All of this is established in authentic *ahaadeeth* and many of these are quoted by al-Haafidh Ibn Katheer in his *tafseer* of verse 159 of Soorah an-Nisaa'. Refer also to *Saheeh al-Bukhaaree* (Eng. trans. vol.4, no.s 657, 658) and *Saheeh Muslim* (Eng. trans. vol.4, no.s 6924,7023).

27 To have Faith that Faith *(Eemaan)* comprises of saying, action and beliefs. It increases and decreases. It increases as Allaah wills and may decrease to the extent that nothing remains of it.[1]

28 The best of this *Ummah* after the passing away of its Prophet is Abu Bakr then 'Umar then 'Uthmaan. This is what is reported to us from Ibn 'Umar who said, *"We used to say whilst Allaah's Messenger (ﷺ) was amongst us: The best of people after the Messenger of Allaah (ﷺ) is Abu Bakr then 'Umar then 'Uthmaan. The Prophet (ﷺ) would hear of that and not criticise it."*[2] Then the best of people after them are 'Alee, Talhah, az-Zubayr, Sa'd ibn Abee Waqqaas, Sa'eed ibn Zayd, 'Abdur-Rahmaan ibn 'Awf and Abu 'Ubaidah 'Aamir ibn al-Jarraah. All of them were suitable to be *Khaleefah*. Then the best of people after them are the (rest of the) Companions of the Messenger of Allaah (ﷺ), the first generation amongst

---

1. Al-Laalikaa'ee reports in *Sharh Usool I'tiqaad Ahl is-Sunnah* (5/958/ no.1737) that 'Abd ar-Razzaq (as-San'aanee) said, "I met seventy Shaikhs, from amongst them are: Ma'mar, al-Awzaa'ee, ath-Thawree, al-Waleed ibn Muhammad al-Qurashee, Yazeed ibn as-Saa'ib, Hammaad ibn Salamah, Hammaad ibn Zayd, Sufyaan ibn 'Uyainah, Shu'ayb ibn Harb, Wakee' ibn al-Jarraah, Maalik ibn Anas, Ibn Abee Laylaa, Isma'eel ibn 'Ayyaash, al-Waleed ibn Muslim and those I have not named, all of them saying: Faith is saying and action, it increases and decreases."

'Abdullaah ibn Ahmad reports in as-*Sunnah* (no.612): My father narrated to me: Abu Salamah al-Khuzaa'ee related to us, saying, "Maalik, Shareek, Abu Bakr ibn 'Ayyaash, 'Abdul-'Azeez ibn Abee Salamah, Hammaad ibn Salamah and Hammaad ibn Zayd said: Faith is conviction, declaration and action."

Al-Laalikaa'ee reports (5/959/no.1740) that 'Uqbah ibn 'Alqamah said: I asked al-Awzaa'ee about Faith. Can it increase? He said, "Yes, until it becomes like the mountains." I said: can it decrease? He said, "Yes, even until nothing remains of it."

Amongst the verses quoted by the scholars as proof for the fact that Faith increases are: *Aayah* 173 of Soorah Aali-'Imraan, *Aayah* 4 of Soorah al-Fath and *Aayah* 124 of Soorah at-Tawbah.

2. This is reported by al-Bukhaaree (5/6/no.7), Ahmad in *Fadaailus-Sahaabah* (no. 570) and *as-Sunnah* 'Abdullaah ibn Ahmad (pp. 574 - 578).

whom he was sent, the first *Muhaajirs* and *Ansaar*, those who prayed towards both *qiblahs* then the best of people after them are those who accompanied the Messenger of Allaah (ﷺ) for a day, a month or a year or less or more than that. We ask Allaah to have mercy upon them. We mention their virtues and remain silent about any mistakes they made and we do not speak about a single one of them except favourably as the Messenger of Allaah (ﷺ) said, *"When my Companions are mentioned then withold."*[1] Sufyaan ibn 'Uyainah[2] said, "He who speaks a single word against the Companions of Allaah's Messenger (ﷺ) then he is an innovator."[3]

29 To hear and obey the rulers in that which Allaah loves and is pleased with. Whoever becomes *Khaleefah* through the consensus of the people and their being pleased with him, then he is the 'Chief of the Believers' (*Ameerul-Mumineen*).

30 It is then not permissible for anyone to spend a single night thinking that he has no Imaam over him whether he be righteous or wicked.

---

1. Saheeh: Reported by at-Tabaraanee from Ibn Mas'ood from the Prophet (ﷺ). See *Silsilatul-Ahaadeethis-Saheehah* (no. 34) of Shaikh al-Albaanee.
2. Shaikhul-Islaam, Sufyaan ibn 'Uyainah was a *Taabi'ut-Taabi'een*. He was born in 107 H, in Makkah and died in 198 H.
3. In the printed edition after the saying of Sufyaan there occurs: The Prophet (ﷺ) said, "My Companions are like stars, whichever of them you follow you will be guided." This narration is a fabrication. Refer to *Silsilatul-Ahaadeethid-Da'eefah* (no. 58) and *The Prophet's Prayer Described* by Shaikh al-Albaanee (pp. 94-96).

31 The *Hajj* and *Jihaad* are to be carried out under his leadership. *Jumu'ah* Prayer behind them (i.e. the wicked rulers)[1] is allowed and after it six *rak'ahs* should be prayed, splitting it into sets of two *rak'ahs*. This is the saying of Ahmad ibn Hanbal.[2]

32 *Khilaafah* will remain within the Quraish until 'Eesaa ibn Maryam, *'alaihis-Salaam*, descends.[3]

33 Whoever rebels against a Muslim ruler is one of the *Khawaarij*,[4] has caused dissent within the Muslims and has contradicted the narrations and dies a death of the days of ignorance *(Jaahiliyyah)*.[5]

---

1. 'Ubaydullaah ibn 'Adiyy ibn Khiyaar reports: I went to 'Uthmaan, *radiallaahu 'anhu*, whilst he was being besieged and said to him: You are the ruler of the Muslims in general and you see what has befallen you. We are being lead in Prayer by a leader of insurrection and are afraid of being sinful. So 'Uthmaan said, "The Prayer is the best of actions which people do, so when the people do good deeds then do good along with them. When they do evil, avoid their evil." Reported by al-Bukhaaree (Eng. trans. 1/376/ch.56).

2. 'Abdullaah ibn Ahmad ibn Hanbal reports in his *Masaail* (no. 446), "I asked my father how many should I pray after *Jumu'ah*? He said: If you wish then pray four *(rak'ahs)* and if you wish pray six *rak'ahs*, in twos, that is what I prefer and if you pray four then there is no harm." Abu Daawood reports in his *Masaail* (p. 59), "I heard Ahmad say: (Regarding) Prayer after *Jumu'ah*, if one prays four, good, if one prays two, good and if one prays six, good."

3. Mu'aawiyah reports that Allaah's Messenger (صلى الله عليه وسلم) said, *"This affair (Khilaafah) will remain with the Quraish. None will rebel against them except that Allaah will throw him down on his face, as long as they establish the Religion."* Reported by al-Bukhaaree (Eng. trans. 9/190/253).

4. The *Khawaarij* are a group who first appeared in the time of 'Alee, *radiallaahu 'anhu*. They split from his army and began the grave innovation of *Takfeer* (declaring Muslims, rulers or the ruled, in their view guilty of major sins, to be disbelievers). The Prophet (صلى الله عليه وسلم) warned against them in many authentic *ahaadeeth*: *"The Khawaarij are the dogs of the Fire."* Reported by Ahmad and is *saheeh*. He (صلى الله عليه وسلم) also informed us that they would continue to appear until the end of this world, saying, *"A group will appear reciting the Qur'aan, it will not pass beyond their throats, every time a group appears it is to be cut off, until the Dajjaal appears within them."* Reported by Ibn Maajah and is *hasan*. Refer to *Silsilatul-Ahaadeethis-Saheehah* (no. 2455).

5. Refer to the *hadeeth* reported by Ibn 'Abbaas, *radiallaahu 'anhummaa*, =

42

34 It is not permissible to fight the ruler nor to rebel against him even if he oppresses. This is due to the saying of the Messenger of Allaah to Abu Dharr al-Ghifaaree, *"Have patience even if he is an Abyssinian slave"*[1] and his (ﷺ) saying to the Ansaar, *"Have patience until you meet me at the Pool."*[2] There is no fighting against the ruler in the *Sunnah*. It causes destruction of the Religion and the worldly affairs.[3]

35 It is permissible to fight the *Khawaarij* if they attack the persons, property or families of the Muslims[4] but if they desist and flee then they may not be chased, nor are their wounded to be killed, nor set upon, nor may those taken captive be killed, nor those who flee to be followed.

36 Know that there is no obedience to any human in disobedience to Allaah, the Mighty and Majestic.[5]

---

mentioned in the footnote to point number two of the book.

1. Its like is reported by Muslim (Eng. trans. vol.3, nos. 4525, 4526).

2. Reported by al-Bukhaaree (Eng. trans. vol.5, no.136) from the *hadeeth* of Usayd ibn al-Hudayr.

3. Hudhaifah, *radiallaahu 'anhu*, reports in a longer *hadeeth* that the Messenger of Allaah (ﷺ) said, *"There will come leaders who will not follow my guidance and will not follow my Sunnah. There will be amongst them men who will have the hearts of devils in the bodies of humans."* He (Hudhaifah) asked, "What shall I do O Messenger of Allaah if I reach that?" He replied, *"You should hear and obey the ruler even if he flogs your back and takes your wealth, then still hear and obey."* Reported by Muslim (Eng. trans. 3/1029/no.4554).

Al-Khallaal reports in as-*Sunnah* (no.87) that Abu Bakr related to us, saying, "I heard Abu 'Abdullaah (Imaam Ahmad) ordering that bloodshed be avoided and he strongly forbade rebellion."

4. Refer to *Saheeh al-Bukhaaree* (Eng. trans. vol.9, pp. 49-53).

5. He (ﷺ) said, *"Obedience is only in what is good."* Reported by al-Bukhaaree (Eng. trans. 9/193/259) and Muslim (Eng. trans. 3/1022/no.4535). He (ﷺ) also said, *"Hearing and obeying is (binding) upon the Muslim in what he likes or dislikes, so long as he is not ordered to sin. If he is ordered with sin, then there is no hearing and no obeying."* Reported by al-Bukhaaree (Eng. trans. 9/193/no.258), Muslim (Eng. trans. 3/1022/no.4533) and Abu Daawood.

37 Do not bear witness for any of the people of Islaam (i.e. that he is a person of Paradise or of the Fire) due to a good or bad deed, since you do not know what his final action before his death will be. You hope for Allaah's Mercy for him and you fear for him because of his sins. You do not know what has been destined for him at the time of his death[1] as regards repentance and what Allaah has destined for that time if he dies upon Islaam. You hope for Allaah's Mercy for him and you fear for him because of his sins.

38 There is no sin except that the servant may repent from it.

39 Stoning is true and correct.[2]

---

1. Al-Miqdaad ibn al-Aswad, *radiallaahu 'anhu,* said: I will not say anything good or bad about a person until I see how he ends, after something I heard from the Prophet (ﷺ). It was said 'What did you hear?' He said: I heard the Messenger of Allaah (ﷺ) say, *"The heart of the son of Aadam is agitated more severely than the cooking pot when it boils."* Reported by Ahmad, al-Haakim and Ibn Abee 'Aasim in *as-Sunnah* (no. 226). Declared *Saheeh* by Shaikh al-Albaanee in *Saheehul-Jaami'* (5023).

Anas, *radiallaahu 'anhu,* reports that the Messenger of Allaah (ﷺ) said, *"Do not be delighted by the action of anyone until you see how he ends up."* Reported by Ahmad and Ibn Abee 'Aasim in *as-Sunnah* (347 - 353) and declared *saheeh* by Shaikh al-Albaanee in *Silsilatul-Ahaadeethis-Saheehah* (no. 1334).

2. This refers to the stoning to death of a man or a woman guilty of fornication, who are or have previously been married.

'Ubaadah ibn as-Saamit reported that the Messenger of Allaah (ﷺ) said, *"Receive from me, receive from me: Allaah has ordained a way for those (women). When an unmarried man commits fornication with an unmarried woman, then one hundred lashes and banishment for one year. As for a married man committing adultery with a married woman then they shall be lashed a hundred times and stoned to death."* Reported by Muslim (Eng. trans. 3/911/no.4191).

40 Wiping over the leather socks (*khuff*) is the *Sunnah*.[1]

41 Shortening the Prayer when travelling is the *Sunnah*.

42 As regards fasting when travelling, whoever wishes may fast and whoever wishes may abstain from fasting.[2]

43 There is no harm in praying whilst wearing broad and loose trousers.[3]

44 Hypocrisy is to display Islaam with the tongue whilst inwardly hiding disbelief.[4]

---

1. Al-Laalikaa'ee reports in *Sharh Usool I'tiqaad Ahl is-Sunnah* (1/no.314/p.152) that Sufyaan ath-Thawree said within the *'Aqeedah* which he narrated to Shu'ayb ibn Harb, ".... O Shu'ayb ibn Harb! What I have written for you will not benefit you until you hold that wiping over leather socks without removing them is better for you than washing the feet..."

2. Shaikh ul-Islam Ibn Taimiyyah, *rahimahullaah,* says in *Majmoo' al-Fatawaa* (25/209), "As regards the journey on which the Prayer may be shortened, it is permissible to abstain from fasting on it and to make up the fast later on, by agreement of the scholars. Abstaining from fasting is allowed for the traveller by agreement of the scholars, whether one is able to fast or not, whether fasting is difficult or not, even if the traveller was shaded, had sufficient water and had someone to serve him, still it is allowed for him to abstain from fasting and to shorten the Prayer. Whoever says that abstaining from fasting is only allowed for one who is unable to fast then repentance is to be sought from him, so either he repents or is executed. Likewise, for one who criticises the one who abstains from fasting (on the journey) then his repentance is to be sought."

3. These points of *fiqh* have been mentioned by the author, since they were matters which were denied by some of the sects of innovation.

4. Hypocrisy (*Nifaaq*) is of two types: (i) Hypocrisy of belief: This is what is mentioned by the author here. This type of hypocrisy takes a person outside the fold of Islaam. (ii) Hypocrisy of action: This involves a person having some of the characteristics of the hypocrites, i.e. lying, breaking promises, proving dishonest when trusted, behaving impudently when disputing and proving treacherous with regards to contracts. This type, although very serious, does not take a person outside of Islaam but in time it may lead to that.

45 Know that the world is the place of *Eemaan* and Islaam.[1]

46 Amongst the nation of Muhammad (ﷺ) are Believers and Muslims with regard to rulings, inheritance, slaughtering animals and funeral prayer.

47 However, we do not bear witness that any of them is a true and perfect Believer, unless he fulfils all the laws and duties of Islaam. If he neglects any of that, then his Faith is deficient until he repents. His Faith is for Allaah, the Most High, alone to judge, whether it is complete or incomplete, except for when any of the duties of Islaam are seen to be neglected.

48 (Funeral) prayer upon anyone who dies from the people of the *Qiblah* is *Sunnah*. The adulterer or adulteress stoned to death, the one who commits suicide, others from the people of the *Qiblah*, the drunkard and other than them, to pray the (funeral) prayer over them is the *Sunnah*.

49 None of the people of the *Qiblah* leave Islaam unless they reject an *Aayah* from the Book of Allaah, the Mighty and Majestic, or reject any narrations from the Messenger of Allaah (ﷺ), or pray to other than Allaah or sacrifice to other than Allaah.[2] If he does any of that, it is binding upon you to expel him from Islaam. If he does not do any of that, he is a Believer and a Muslim in name, even if not in reality.

---

1. The majority of scholars hold that this world is divided between *Daarul-Islaam* and *Daarul-Kufr*.

2. Or directing any part or form of worship to other than Allaah. For example, performing *tawaaf* around graves, supplicating to the dead, seeking assistance or relief from the dead. If a person does any of these actions in ignorance, those with knowledge should teach him that this is *Shirk* and establish the proof against him, so that he is able to understand it, but if he then arrogantly rejects it and continues in *Shirk* knowingly, he has left Islaam.

50 Everything of the narrations which you heard but cannot fully understand, like the saying of the Messenger of Allaah (ﷺ), *"The hearts of the servants are between two Fingers of the Most Merciful, the Mighty and Majestic,"*[1] his (ﷺ) saying, *"Indeed Allaah descends to the lowest heaven,"*[2] *"He descends on the Day of 'Arafah,"*[3] *"He descends on the Day of Resurrection,"*[4] *"Hellfire does not cease having them thrown into it until He, the Majestic, places His Foot upon it,"*[5] Allaah, the Most High's, saying to the servant, *"If you walk towards Me, I run towards you,"*[6] his (ﷺ) saying, *"Allaah created Aadam in his image,"*[7] the saying of Allaah's Messenger (ﷺ), *"I saw my Lord in*

---

1. Reported by Muslim (Eng. trans. 4/1397/no.6418) and Ahmad.

2. The *hadeeth* about Allaah descending is authentic and has many routes of narration. For example, refer to al-Bukhaaree (Eng. trans. 2/136/no.246) and Muslim (Eng. trans. 1/365/no.1656).

3. He (ﷺ) said, *"Allaah descends on the evening of 'Arafah to the lowest heaven and boasts about the people of the earth to the Angels."* Reported by Ibn Mandah in *at-Tawheed* (147/1). Its chain of narration is weak as explained in *Silsilatud-Da'eefah* (no.679) of Shaikh al-Albaanee. However, it is authentic as the saying of Umm Salamah, *radilallaahu 'anhaa*, reported by ad-Daarimee in *ar-Radd 'alal-Jahmiyyah*, ad-Daaraqutnee in *an-Nuzool* (95,96) and al-Laalikaa'ee (no.768). It has the ruling of being the saying of the Prophet (ﷺ) since it is something which Umm Salamah could not have known except from him (ﷺ).

4. Refer to *ar-Radd 'alal-Jahmiyyah* of ad-Daarimee (p.72). Allaah, the Most High, says:

$$\text{وَجَآءَ رَبُّكَ وَٱلۡمَلَكُ صَفًّا صَفًّا ۝}$$

Your Lord comes with His angels, rank upon rank.

Soorah al-Fajr (89):22

5. Reported by al-Bukhaaree (Eng. trans. 6/353/no.371) and Muslim (Eng. trans. 4/1483/no.6819).

6. Reported by al-Bukhaaree (Eng. trans. 9/369/no.502) and Muslim (Eng. trans. 4/1408/no.6471).

7. Reported by Muslim (Eng. trans. 4/1378/no.6325) and Ibn Abee 'Aasim in *as-Sunnah*. Explanation of this *hadeeth*, by Shaikh Hammaad al-Ansaaree can be found in *Kitaabus-Sifaat* of ad-Daaraqutnee (p.58, checking of Dr. 'Alee Naasir Faqeehee).

47

the most excellent form"[1] and the like of these *ahaadeeth*, then accept them, affirm them, perform *Tafweed*[2] (i.e. abandon delving into how they are) (but be pleased with them). Do not explain any of them with your feelings/desires, since believing in them is obligatory. So anyone who explains anything from them according to his desires or rejects them is a *Jahmee*.[3]

---

1. *Musnad Ahmad* (1/285 and 290) and Ibn Abee 'Aasim in *as-Sunnah* and declared *saheeh* by Shaikh al-Albaanee who has mentioned that, "this was in a dream as indicated by some wordings (of the *hadeeth*)." Refer, also to *as-Sunnah* (no. 1117) of 'Abdullaah ibn Ahmad.

2. *Tafweed*: The *Salaf* did not delve into 'how' the attributes of Allaah are. The knowledge of that is with Allaah alone. But, as for the *Ash'arees* and others, *'Tafweed'* to them is that they believe that what is apparent from the attributes is not what is meant. To them the *Aayaat* about the attributes of Allaah are *mutashaabih* i.e. of uncertain meaning and thus they were not known about by the Prophet (ﷺ) and the Companions. This is clearly wrong! Refer to *Risaalah 'Alaaqatul-Ithbaat wat-Tafweed bi Siffat Rabbil-'Aalameen* of Dr. Ridaa Mu'tee and Shaikh 'Abdul-'Azeez ibn Baaz, *hafdhahullaah's*, reply to as-Saaboonee (pp.8-14).

3. *Jahmee*: a denier of Allaah's attributes, following the way al-Jahm ibn Safwaan and his teacher al-Ja'd ibn Dirham, both of whom were executed for their wicked beliefs and heretical teachings.

The correct belief with regards to the attributes of Allaah is the belief of *Ahl us-Sunnah wal-Jamaa'ah*. That is, we have Faith in all of Allaah's attributes without denying them or their meanings (*ta'teel*), without interpreting them and changing their meaning (*tahreef*), without explaining how they are (*takyeef*) or likening Allaah's attributes to those of the creation (*tamtheel*).

48

51 Anyone who claims to have seen his Lord in this world is a Disbeliever in Allaah, the Mighty and Majestic.[1]

52 Reflecting deeply about Allaah is an innovation, as Allaah's Messenger (ﷺ) said, *"Reflect upon the creation and do not reflect upon Allaah,"*[2] since trying to reflect deeply about Allaah causes doubt in the heart.

53 Know that reptiles, beasts of prey and all creatures such as the tiny ant, the fly and the ant are all acting as they are commanded. They do not do anything except by the permission of Allaah, the Blessed and the Most High.

---

1. i.e. One who claims to have seen Allaah whilst awake. Perhaps he is referring to the extreme *Soofees* and those who claim that Allaah is within His creation or that it is possible to become at one with or annihilated with Allaah or to those who claim that they have received knowledge and inspiration direct from Allaah. High is Allaah above and far removed from the claims they make.

2. Reported with this wording by Abush-Shaikh in *al-'Azamah* (no.5) and Abul-Qaasim al-Asbahaanee in *at-Targheeb* (2/73;174) from the *marfoo' hadeeth* of Ibn 'Abbaas and its *isnaad* is weak. However, it has a witness in the *hadeeth* of 'Abdullaah ibn Sallaam in *marfoo'* form reported by Abu Nu'aym in *al-Hilyah* (6/66-67) which brings it to the level of *hasan*. It has further witnesses which are weak. Refer to *Silsilatus-Saheehah* (no.1788).

The reflection which is forbidden here is to try to reflect about Allaah's Self, asking 'how?' and, 'why?' and so on. The *hadeeth* is also a reply to those who claim that the first obligation upon a person is to have doubt, or to reflect and ponder. However, it is not forbidden to reflect on Allaah's creation, His dominion, the blessings which He has bestowed, His Greatness and His names and attributes.

54 To have Faith that Allaah knew whatever would be from the start of time and whatever would not be and that He fully enumerated and comprehended everything that was to be. Anyone who says, 'He did not know that which was or will be in existence,'[1] has disbelieved in Allaah, the Most Sublime.

55 There is no marriage except with a guardian (*Walee*)[2] and two just witnesses and a dower (*Sadaaq/Mahr*) whether it is a small amount or a large amount. As for a woman without a guardian, then the ruler is the guardian of one without a guardian.

56 If a man divorces his wife three times, she is forbidden to him. (She) is not permissible for him unless she marries another man.[3]

57 The blood of a Muslim who bears witness that none has the right to be worshipped but Allaah and that Muhammad (ﷺ) is His slave and Messenger may not be spilt except in three cases: fornication after having been married, apostasy after Faith or one who kills a Believer without right and so is executed for it. Apart from that the Muslim's blood is unlawful forever, until the Last Hour is established.[4]

---

1. This is the saying of Hishaam ibn al-Hakam, the leader of misguidance, who believed that Allaah, the Most Perfect, did not know anything until He created knowledge of it for Himself. This is clear disbelief.

2. Abu Moosa reported that the Prophet (ﷺ) said, *"There is no marriage without the guardian (walee)."* Reported by Abu Daawood (Eng. trans. 2/558/no.2080) and is *saheeh*.

3. The *Salaf* would sometimes include matters of *fiqh* in their works on *'Aqeedah* if they were matters where clear texts were present yet people still held views contrary to these texts.

4. The wording of the *hadeeth* is, *"The blood of a Muslim, who witnesses that none has the right to be worshipped except Allaah and that Muhammad is the Messenger of Allaah, is not lawful except in three (cases): The married fornicator, a life for a life and the one who abandons his Religion and leaves the Jamaa'ah."* Reported by al-Bukhaaree (Eng. trans. 9/10/no.17) and Muslim (Eng. trans. 3/898/no.4152).

58 Everything which Allaah has decreed will come to an end will indeed end. Paradise and the Fire will not end, nor the Throne (*'Arsh*), the Footstool (*Kursee*), the Pen (*Qalam*), the Horn (*Soor*), and the Preserved Tablet (*Lawh*). None of these will ever perish. Then Allaah will raise up the creation on the Day of Resurrection in the state in which He caused them to die. He will take account of them as He pleases, a group for Paradise and a group for the burning Fire and He will say to the rest of creation which were not created to last: "Be dust."

59 To have Faith in the retribution (*Qisaas*) on the Day of Resurrection, between all of creation: humans, reptiles, beasts of prey and even between ants, until Allaah, the Mighty and Majestic, brings about justice for all of them from each other, the people of Paradise from the people of the Fire, the people of the Fire from the people of Paradise, the people of Paradise from each other and the people of the Fire from each other.[1]

60 To make actions purely and sincerely for Allaah.

---

1. There occurs in the *hadeeth*, "*It is not fitting for any of the people of Paradise to enter Paradise, whilst there is a right due from him to a person of the people of the Fire, until I exact retribution from him for him, even a slap.*" We said: How when we are to come before Allaah, the Mighty and Majestic, barefooted, uncircumcised and naked? He said, "*With good and bad deeds.*" Reported by Ahmad, al-Bukhaaree in *al-Adabul-Mufrad* (no. 970) and al-Haakim declared it *saheeh* and adh-Dhahabee agreed. Shaikh al-Albaanee declared the *hadeeth* to be *hasan*.

61 To be pleased with the decree of Allaah, to have patience with the Judgement of Allaah, to believe in whatever Allaah, the Mighty and Majestic, has said and to believe in all that Allaah has pre-decreed, the good and the bad, and the sweet and the bitter. Allaah knew what the servants were going to do and to where they were heading. They cannot escape the Knowledge of Allaah. There is nothing in the earths or in the heavens except that Allaah, the Most High, knows it. You should know that whatever befalls you was never going to miss you and whatever you missed was never going to befall you.[1] There is no creator besides Allaah, the Mighty and Majestic.[2]

---

1. There occurs in the *hadeeth* narrated by Ibn 'Abbaas, *"..know that if the Ummah gathered together to benefit you with something, then they could not benefit you, unless Allaah had written it down for you and if they gathered to harm you with something then they could not do so, unless Allaah had written it down for you. The pens have been raised and the scrolls dried."* Reported by at-Tirmidhee (no. 2518) who declared it *hasan-saheeh.* Refer to *an-Nawawee's Forty Hadeeth* (no.19).

To have Faith in Allaah's pre-decree (*Qadr*) is one of the pillars of Faith. Whoever rejects it is not a Believer. It has four principles: (i) That Allaah knew everything that would ever be. (ii) That Allaah wrote everything that would ever be in the Preserved Tablet. (iii) That Allaah willed whatever occurs. (iv) That Allaah created everything. For a more detailed explanation of these principles refer to *Faith in Predestination* edited by Dr. Suhaib Hasan.

2. This is to emphasise that Allaah creates everything including man's actions. Unlike, the *Qadariyyah* (the deniers of *Qadr*), who believe that man creates his own actions, just as the Magians believed in two creators; a creator of good and a creator of evil. The Prophet (ﷺ) foretold the appearance of this sect, when he said, *"The Qadariyyah are the Magians of this ummah. If they fall ill, do not visit them and if they die then do not attend their funeral."* Reported by Abu Daawood. Shaikh al-Albaanee declares the *hadeeth* to be *hasan* in *Saheeh ul-Jaami'.* Concerning a person's actions, Allaah, the Most High, says:

Allaah created you and your actions.

Soorah Saffaat (37):96

=

52

62 Four *Takbeers* are to be said for the *Janaazah* Prayer. This is the saying of Maalik ibn Anas, Sufyaan ath-Thawree, al-Hasan ibn Saalih, Ahmad ibn Hanbal and the scholars and it was the saying of the Messenger of Allaah (ﷺ).[1]

63 To have Faith that with every raindrop there is an angel who descends with it until he places it where Allaah, the Mighty and Majestic, has ordered.[2]

64 To have Faith that when the Messenger of Allaah (ﷺ) spoke to the (dead) people thrown into the dry well on the Day of Badr (i.e. the *mushriks*) they heard his words.[3]

Allaah alone is the creator of everything, including man's actions. However, He gave man limited free-will to choose between good and evil. Furthermore He, the Most High, sent His Messengers to call to goodness and to that which leads to Paradise and to warn against evil and that which leads to Hell-Fire. So man earns and is fully responsible for his own actions. Imaam al-Bukhaaree wrote a whole book entitled *Khalq Af'aal ul-'Ibaad* (The actions of the servants are created) on this subject.

1. Al-Bukhaaree (Eng. trans. 2/233/no.417) and Muslim (Eng. trans. 2/453/no.2084) both report that he (ﷺ) said four *takbeers* over an-Najjaashee. Refer to *Ahkaamul-Janaaiz* of Shaikh al-Albaanee (p. 111) and the book *Death* by 'Alee Hasan 'Abdul-Hameed may be referred to for funeral regulations.

2. This is reported as the saying of al-Hakam ibn 'Utaibah *(taabi'ee*, died 115H) reported by at-Tabaree in his *Tafseer* (14/19) with a *hasan isnaad*. It is also reported as the saying of al-Hasan al-Basree (d.110H) by Abush-Shaikh in *al-'Azamah* (no.761) with a *hasan isnaad*.

3. *The Prophet (ﷺ) called out, "O Abu Jahl ibn Hishaam! O Umayyah ibn Khalaf! O 'Utbah ibn Rabee'ah! O Shaibah ibn Rabee'ah" and he named their heads, "Have you found what your Lord promised you to be true? Because I have found what my Lord promised me to be true!" 'Umar said, "O Messenger of Allaah! You speak to a people who have become corpses?" So he replied, "By Him in whose Hand is my soul! You do not hear what I am saying better than they, but they are unable to reply."* Reported by al-Bukhaaree (Eng. trans. 5/209/no.314) and Muslim (Eng. trans. 4/1491/no.6869).

65 To have Faith that if a man becomes ill, Allaah rewards him for his illness.[1]

66 (To have Faith) that Allaah rewards the martyr for his death.

67 To have Faith that children feel pain if afflicted in this world. Bakr,[2] the son of the sister of Abdil-Waahid, said, 'They do not feel pain.' He has lied.

68 Know that no-one will enter Paradise except through the Mercy of Allaah. Allaah will not punish anyone except according to the degree of his sins. If He were to punish them all, the inhabitants of the heavens and earths, the good and the bad of them, then He would punish them without being unjust to them.[3]

It is not permissible to describe Allaah, the Most High, as being unjust, since the unjust is the one who takes that which is not his own, whereas creation and decree belong to Allaah, the Magnificent. The creation is His creation and the world is His.

---

1. 'Abdullaah ibn Mas'ood reports: I visited the Prophet (ﷺ) during his illness and he was suffering from a high fever. I said, 'You have a high fever. Is it because you will have a double reward for it?' He replied, *"Yes, no Muslim is afflicted by harm except that Allaah removes his sins, just as the leaves fall off a tree."* Reported by al-Bukhaaree (Eng. trans. 7/373/no.550) and Muslim (Eng. trans. 4/1364/no.6235).

2. This Bakr was one of the heads of innovation. His biography can be found in *Lisaan ul-Meezaan* (2/60-61) of Ibn Hajr.

3. Ubayy ibn K'ab reports that the Prophet (ﷺ) said, *"If Allaah punished those who inhabit His Heavens and His earth, He would punish them without being unjust to them. If He had Mercy upon them, His mercy would be greater than their actions."* Reported by Abu Daawood, Ibn Maajah and Ahmad. The *hadeeth* is declared *saheeh* by Shaikh al-Albaanee in *Saheehul-Jaami'* (no. 5244).

He is not to be questioned about what He does but they are to be questioned. 'Why?' and 'How?' are not asked. None can enter between Allaah and His creation.[1]

69 If you hear a man criticising the narrations, not accepting them or rejecting any of the narrations from the Messenger of Allaah (ﷺ), doubt his Islaam since he is a person having a despicable opinion and saying. He is indeed attacking the Messenger of Allaah (ﷺ) and his Companions, since we have only come to know of Allaah, His Messenger (ﷺ), the Qur'aan, what is good and bad and of this world and the Hereafter through the narrations.[2]

---

1. No one may be taken as an intermediary since Allaah hears the supplication of whoever calls upon Him. Moreover, Allaah is not in need of any intermediaries. Allaah, the Most High, says:

$$\text{وَإِذَا سَأَلَكَ عِبَادِى عَنِّى فَإِنِّى قَرِيبٌ أُجِيبُ دَعْوَةَ ٱلدَّاعِ إِذَا دَعَانِ}$$

$$\text{فَلْيَسْتَجِيبُوا لِى وَلْيُؤْمِنُوا بِى لَعَلَّهُمْ يَرْشُدُونَ ﴿١٨٦﴾}$$

When My slaves ask you concerning Me, (answer them), I am indeed near. I respond to the invocations of the supplicant when he calls on Me. So let them obey Me and believe in Me, so that they may be led aright.

Soorah al-Baqarah (2):186

$$\text{وَقَالَ رَبُّكُمُ ٱدْعُونِى أَسْتَجِبْ لَكُمْ}$$

Your Lord says: Call on Me; I will answer your (Prayer).

Soorah Ghaafir (40):60

2. The Prophet (ﷺ) said, *"There will come a time, when a man sitting upon his couch is mentioned a hadeeth and he replies, 'Between us and you is the Book of Allaah, the Mighty and Majestic, so what we find in it to be lawful we take it as lawful and what we find in it to forbidden we take it to be forbidden.' Indeed what the Messenger of Allaah has forbidden is like what Allaah has forbidden."* Reported by Ahmad, Abu Daawood, Ibn Maajah and at-Tirmidhee who declared it *hasan*. Al-Albaanee declared it *saheeh* in *Saheehul-Jaami'* (no.8186). =

55

70 The Qur'aan needs the *Sunnah* more than the *Sunnah* needs the Qur'aan.[1]

71 (Unwarranted) speech, argumentation and disputation about Pre-decree is forbidden with all the sects, since Pre-decree is Allaah's secret. The Lord, the Blessed and Most High, forbade the Prophets from (such) speech about it. The Prophet (ﷺ) forbade argumentation about Pre-decree; the Companions of Allaah's Messenger (ﷺ) and the Successors hated it. It was hated by the scholars and the people of piety; they forbade disputation about Pre-decree. So submit, affirm, have Faith and believe in what Allaah's Messenger (ﷺ) said about matters and remain silent concerning other than that.

Imaam Maalik, *rahimahullaah*, said, "Everyone after the Prophet (ﷺ) will have his saying accepted or rejected, not so the Prophet (ﷺ)." Reported by Ibn 'Abdul-Barr in *Jaami' Bayaan al-'Ilm* (2/91).

Imaam Ahmad, *rahimahullaah*, said, "Whoever rejects a *hadeeth* of Allaah's Messenger (ﷺ) is on the brink of destruction." Reported in *Tabaqaatul-Hanaabliah* (2/15) and by Ibn Battah in *al-Ibaanatul-Kubraa* (1/97).

1. This saying of al-Barbahaaree, *rahimahullaah*, is also reported as the saying of Makhool ash-Shaamee, the *taabi'ee* (d.113H) by al-Khateeb in *al-Kifaayah* (p.14) and others with a *saheeh* chain of narration.

Yahyaa ibn Abee Katheer, the *taabi'ee*, (d.129H) said, "The *Sunnah* is decisive over the Qur'aan, but the Qur'aan is not decisive over the *Sunnah*." Reported by ad-Daarimee in *as-Sunan* (1/153).

Al-Fudayl ibn Ziyaad said: I heard Abu 'Abdullaah, meaning Ahmad ibn Hanbal, being asked about the narration, that the *Sunnah* is decisive over the Book, so he said, "I do not venture to say that the *Sunnah* is decisive over the Book but the *Sunnah* does explain the Book and clarifies it." Reported by Ibn 'Abdul-Barr in *al-Jaami'* (pp.191-192). This agrees with Allaah's Saying:

$$\text{وَأَنزَلْنَا إِلَيْكَ ٱلذِّكْرَ لِتُبَيِّنَ لِلنَّاسِ مَا نُزِّلَ إِلَيْهِمْ}$$

We have revealed to you the Reminder (the Qur'aan), so that you may explain clearly to men, what is sent down to them.

Soorah an-Nahl (16):44

72. To have Faith that the Messenger of Allaah (ﷺ) was taken by night up through the heavens and came to the Throne and spoke to Allaah, the Blessed and Most High, and entered Paradise and saw into the Fire and saw the angels [and heard the Speech of Allaah, the Mighty and Majestic, and the Prophets were shown to him]. He saw the drapery of the Throne, the Footstool (*Kursee*) and all within the heavens and the earths whilst awake, being taken by Jibreel upon al-Buraaq,[1] who took him through the heavens. That night the five daily Prayers were obligated for him. He returned to Makkah that same night and that was before the *Hijrah*.[2]

73 Know that the souls of martyrs are within the bellies of green birds which roam freely around Paradise and nest in lamps beneath the Throne.[3] The souls of the Believers are beneath the Throne.[4] The souls of the disbelievers and the wicked are within the well of *Barahoot* and are in *Sijjeen*.[5]

---

1. Anas reports that the Messenger of Allaah (ﷺ) said, *"I was brought al-Buraaq, an animal, which was white and long, larger than a donkey but smaller than a mule. It would place its hoof at the distance equal to the range of one's vision..."* Reported by Muslim (Eng. trans. 1/100/no.309).

2. The *hadeeth* of al-Israa' is firmly established and is reported by al-Bukhaaree (Eng. trans. 4/287/no.429) and Muslim (Eng. trans. 3/1029/no.4554). As-Suyootee compiled a treatise in which he brought together the different narrations about al-Israa' and he called it al-Aayaatul-Kubraa fee Sharh Qissatil-Israa'.

3. 'Abdullaah ibn Mas'ood reports that the Prophet (ﷺ) said, *"Their souls are within green birds having lanterns suspended from the Throne, roaming freely in Paradise as they please, then taking shelter in those lanterns."* Reported by Muslim (Eng. trans. 3/1047/no.4651).

4. Ka'b ibn Maalik reports that Allaah's Messenger (ﷺ) said, *"The soul of the Believer is (within) a bird amongst the trees of Paradise, until Allaah returns it to his body on the Day when He resurrects him."* Reported by Maalik, Ahmad, at-Tirmidhee and an-Nasaa'ee. Shaikh al-Albaanee has declared it *saheeh* in as-Saheehah (no.995).

5. There is a report that 'Abdullaah ibn 'Amr said, "The souls of the infidels are gathered in *Barahoot,* a deep pit in Hadramaut."   =

74 To have Faith that the deceased is made to sit up in his grave, that Allaah returns his soul to him and that (he) is questioned by *Munkar* and *Nakeer* about Faith and its requisites. Then his soul is drawn out without any pain. The deceased knows the one who visits him when he comes to him.[1] The Believer is made comfortable and blessed in his grave and the wicked is punished as Allaah wills.[2]

75 Know that (......)[3] with the decree and predestination of Allaah.

However, one of the narrators is unknown. The fact that this is not correct is shown clearly in *ar-Rooh* (pp.145-147) of Ibn al-Qayyim and *Ahwaalul-Quboor* (pp.255-263) of Ibn Rajab. Rather, the correct position is that which is indicated by the Book and the *Sunnah*, which is that they are in *Sijjeen* (beneath the seventh earth). Refer to *Mysteries of the Soul Expounded* by Abu Bilal Mustafa al-Kanadi.

1. However, that which is established in the texts is: (i) That the dead hear the footsteps of those departing after the burial (*Saheeh al-Bukhaaree*, Eng. trans. 2/257/no.456), since his soul is returned to his body at this time and he is questioned. (ii) That on the day of Badr the dead pagans in the pit heard the Prophet (ﷺ) addressing them (*Saheeh al-Bukhaaree*, Eng. trans. 9/193/no.258). The greetings of *salaam* given to the dead when visiting the graveyard reaches them, but Allaah knows how. We do not speak about or affirm any of the affairs of the unseen (*al-ghayb*) except with a text from either the Book or the Sunnah.

2. As reported by al-Bukhaaree (Eng. trans. 2/254-260/nos.450-461), Muslim (Eng. trans. 4/1489-1491/nos.6857-6870) and Ahmad (3/126). Refer to the long hadeeth of al-Baraa' ibn 'Aazib quoted by Shaikh 'Alee Hasan 'Alee 'Abdul-Hameed in the book *Death* (pp.12-19).

3. The checker, Khaalid ar-Radaadee wrote in his footnote to this work, "A word in one manuscript which I am unable to decipher and this sentence is not found in the other manuscript."

76 To have Faith that it was Allaah, the Blessed and Most High, who spoke to Moosaa ibn 'Imraan on the Day of Mount Toor and that Moosaa heard Allaah's Speech, a Voice which he heard from Him, not from other than Him. He who says other than this has disbelieved in Allaah, the Sublime.[1]

---

1. Shaikh ul-Islaam Ibn Taimiyyah said, "The reports are abundant from the Prophet (ﷺ), the Companions, the *taabi'een* and the scholars of *Ahl us-Sunnah* after them that He, the Most Perfect, calls with a Voice. He called upon Moosaa and will call upon His servants on the Day of Resurrection with a Voice. He speaks the Revelation with a Voice. It is not reported from a single one of the *Salaf* that he said, 'Allaah speaks without a voice,' or without words, nor that anyone denied that Allaah speaks with a Voice and with words." (*Al-Majmoo' ul-Fatawaa*, 12/304-305).

'Abdullaah ibn Ahmad reports in *as-Sunnah* (no.532): I asked my father (Imaam Ahmad) about a people who say that when Allaah, the Mighty and Majestic, spoke to Moosaa, He did not speak with a Voice. So my father said, "Rather, your Lord, the Mighty and Majestic, did speak with a voice. We relate these *ahaadeeth*, just as they are reported."

'Abdullaah ibn Ahmad reports in *as-Sunnah* (no.535): I heard Abu Ma'mar al-Hudhalee say, "Whoever claims that Allaah, the Mighty and Majestic, does not speak, nor hear, nor see, nor become angry, nor be pleased, (and he mentioned some attributes) then he is a disbeliever in Allaah, the Mighty and Majestic. If you see him standing by a well, throw him into it. This is what I hold as my Religion before Allaah, the Mighty and Majestic, since they are disbelievers in Allaah, the Most High."

Al-Aajuree says in *ash-Sharee'ah* (p.75), "May Allaah have mercy upon us and you. Know that the saying of the Muslims whose hearts have not deviated from the truth and those who were guided to what is correct in the past and the present is that the Qur'aan is the Speech of Allaah, the Mighty and Majestic. It is not created, since the Qur'aan is from the Knowledge of Allaah, the Most High. The Knowledge of Allaah, the Mighty and Majestic, is not created. High is Allaah, the Mighty and Majestic, above that. This is proven by the Qur'aan, the *Sunnah*, the sayings of the Companions, *radiallaahu ta'aalaa 'anhum*, and the sayings of the scholars of the Muslims, *rahimatullaahi ta'aalaa 'alaihim*. It is not denied except by a filthy *Jahmee*. In the view of the scholars, the *Jahmiyyah* are disbelievers."

Refer to point number 15 of this book, along with the accompanying footnotes.

77 Intellect is inborn. Every person is given the intellect that Allaah wills. They vary in intellect just like a speck (at various heights) in the heavens. Action is sought from each person in accordance with the intellect he has been given.[1] Intellect is not acquired, rather it is a blessing from Allaah, the Blessed and Most High.

78 Know that Allaah has given excellence to the servants, some of them over others in the Religion and worldly affairs. He has done so justly. It is not to be said that He acts unjustly or shows undue favour. Whoever says that Allaah has blessed the Believer and the disbeliever equally is an innovator. Rather Allaah has granted excellence to the Believer over the disbeliever, to the obedient over the sinner and to the innocent over the despicable, doing so justly. It is His Bounty which He grants to whomsoever He pleases and withholds from whomsoever He pleases.

79 It is not permissible to hide sincere advice from any of the Muslims, whether pious or impious, in matters of the Religion. Whoever hides that has acted deceitfully towards the Muslims. Whoever acts deceitfully to the Muslims has done so towards the Religion. Whoever acts deceitfully towards the Religion has behaved treacherously towards Allaah, His Messenger and the Believers.[2]

---

1. Allaah does not call to account or punish the insane. It is authentically reported that the Messenger of Allaah (ﷺ) said, *"The Pen is raised up from three, from the insane whose mind is deranged until he is cured, from the sleeping until he awakes and from the child until he attains puberty."* Reported by Abu Daawood (Eng. trans. 3/1227/no.4388), Ahmad and al-Haakim.

2. Tameem ad-Daaree narrates: The Messenger of Allaah (ﷺ) said, *"The Religion is sincerity."* Upon this we asked, 'To whom?' He replied, *"To Allaah, His Book, His Messenger and to the leaders of the Muslims and their common folk."* Reported by Muslim (Eng. trans. 1/37/no.98).

80 Allaah, the Blessed and Most High, hears, sees and knows. His two Hands are outstretched.[1] He knew that the creation would disobey Him, before He had created them. His Knowledge is effective/operative upon them but His Knowledge of them did not prevent Him from guiding them to Islaam. He blessed them with it out of His generosity, liberality and favour, so all praise is for Him.

81 Know that there are three forms of address of tidings given when one dies. It may be said, 'Receive good tidings, O beloved one of Allaah, of Allaah's pleasure and of Paradise.' It may be said, 'Receive evil tidings, O enemy of Allaah, of Allaah's Anger and the Fire.' It may be said, 'Receive tidings, O servant of Allaah, of Paradise due to Islaam.' This is the saying of Ibn 'Abbaas.[2]

---

1. With regard to the attributes of Allaah, the following must be observed:
(i) We affirm any attribute which Allaah affirmed for Himself or which His Messenger (ﷺ) affirmed for Him.
(ii) We have Faith in the meaning of the attribute.
(iii) We have Faith that this meaning is not in any way like the attributes of the creation.
(iv) The knowledge of how the attributes are is with Allaah alone.
2. As is mentioned in *Tafseer Ibn Katheer* (2/531-538).

82 Know that the first to see Allaah, the Most High, in Paradise are the blind,[1] then the men, then the women. (They) will see (Allaah) with their physical eyes, just as Allaah's Messenger (ﷺ) said, *"Indeed you will see your Lord just as you see the moon on the night it is full. You will have no difficulty in seeing Him."*[2] It is obligatory to believe in this, to deny it is disbelief.

83 May Allaah have mercy upon you! Know that heresy, disbelief, doubts, innovations, misguidance and confusion about the Religion have never occurred except through theological rhetoric (*Kalaam*) and because of the people of theological rhetoric, argumentation, debating and disputation. How can a man plunge into argumentation, disputation and debating seeing that Allaah, the Most High, has said:

None dispute regarding the *Ayaat* (revelations, signs, proofs) of Allaah except those who disbelieve.[3]

You should submit to and be pleased with the narrations and the people of narrations, withhold and remain silent.

---

1. This occurs in a *hadeeth* reported from the Prophet (ﷺ) which is not authentic. It is mentioned by ad-Daylamee in *Firdawsul-Akhbaar* (1/55) from Samurah ibn Jundub, reporting it in *marfoo'* form. It is also reported by al-Laalikaa'ee in *as-Sunnah* (no.924) with a weak *isnaad* from al-Hasan al-Basree, as his own saying.

2. Reported by al-Bukhaaree (Eng. trans. 1/310/no.529), Muslim (Eng. trans. 1/307/no.1322), Abu Daawood (Eng. trans. 3/1324/no.4711) and 'Abdullaah ibn Ahmad in *as-Sunnah* (no. 412). The *hadeeth* does not mention that men will see Allaah before the women.

3. Soorah Ghaafir (40):4

84 To have Faith that Allaah, the Blessed and Most High, will punish the creation in the Fire, in shackles, fetters and chains. The Fire will be inside them, above them and below them. Whereas, the *Jahmiyyah*, from among them Hishaam al-Footee[1] said, 'Rather Allaah will punish them near the Fire.' Thus rejecting (the saying of) Allaah and His Messenger.

85 Know that the obligatory Prayers are five; there being no increase in them nor decrease when prayed in their stated times. On a journey they are two *rak'ahs* except for the *Maghrib* Prayer. Anyone who says that there are more than five (Prayers) has innovated.[2] Allaah will not accept any of them except within their times, except for one who forgets,[3] he is excused and must pray when he remembers or the traveller who may combine the two Prayers,[4] if he wishes.

86 *Zakaah* is to be paid upon gold, silver, dates, grain and cattle as the Messenger of Allaah (ﷺ) has described. He may distribute it or give it to the ruler. Both of these are allowed.

---

1. He is Hishaam ibn 'Amr, a companion of Abul-Hudhail - a caller to the heresy of the *Mu'tazilah*. See *Lisaanul-Meezaan* (6/195) and *al-Fisal* (5/62) of Ibn Hazm.

2. If the author means innovation that amounts to disbelief, that is what is correct, since adding an extra Prayer, for example, is to prescribe an action within the *Sharee'ah* and this is the right of Allaah alone. Anyone who competes with Allaah in that is a disbeliever by the agreement of the scholars.

3. Likewise, one who is asleep as occurs in the *hadeeth*, *"Whoever forgets a Prayer or sleeps through it, its expiation is that he prays it when he remembers."* Reported by Muslim (Eng. trans. 1/335/no.1456).

4. i.e. he may combine the two daytime Prayers, *Dhur* and *'Asr*, together. Likewise he may combine the two night Prayers, *Maghrib* and *'Ishaa*.

87 Know that the beginning of Islaam is the testification that none has the right to be worshipped except Allaah and that Muhammad is His slave and Messenger.[1]

88 Whatever Allaah says is just as He says. There is nothing to contradict what He says. He is as He says.[2]

89 To have Faith in all the laws and whatever is contained in the *Sharee'ah*.

90 Know that buying and selling is lawful if conducted in the markets of the Muslims in accordance with the Book and the *Sunnah*, as long as no deception, oppression or treachery are committed, nor anything in contradiction to the Qur'aan or what is known.

---

1. This is the first obligation upon a person. The declaration of Faith comprises a negation of worship of anything or anyone besides Allaah, that one will worship Allaah alone and that one will only worship Allaah, according to the manner prescribed by the Messenger Muhammad (ﷺ). The conditions for this declaration are seven:
(i) Knowledge of its meaning, what it denies and affirms.
 (ii) Certainty of it.
(iii) Full acceptance of its meaning.
(iv) Submission to it and what it demands.
(v) Truthfulness, such that one's heart agrees with one's saying.
(vi) Purity of intention.
(vii) Loving it and whatever it necessitates, loving the people who adhere to it and hating whatever contradicts it.
2. Allaah, the Most High, says:

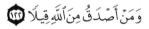

Whose word can be truer than Allaah's?

Soorah an-Nisaa' (4):122

91 May Allaah have mercy upon you! Know that the servant should always have caution and fear, for as long as he remains in this world, since he does not know how he will die, upon what state he will end and upon what condition he will meet Allaah, the Mighty and Majestic, even if he performed every good deed.[1]

92 It is right that any man who transgresses beyond bounds to the detriment of his own soul should not give up hope at the point of death but should think well of Allaah, whilst fearing for his sins.[2] If Allaah has mercy upon him, it is from His bounty. If He punishes him, it is for his sins.

93 To have Faith that Allaah, the Blessed and Most High, showed his Prophet (ﷺ) what was to occur to his *Ummah* until the Day of Resurrection.[3]

---

1. Allaah, the Most High, says:

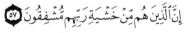

Those who live in awe for fear of their Lord.

Soorah al-Mu'minoon (23):57

2. Anas, *radiallaahu 'anhu*, reports: The Prophet (ﷺ) entered upon a youth who was dying and said, *"How are you?"* He replied 'O Messenger of Allaah! I have hope in Allaah and I fear for my sins.' So Allaah's Messenger (ﷺ) said, *"They do not come together in the heart of a servant in the like of this state except that Allaah gives him what he hopes for and saves him from what he fears."* Reported by at-Tirmidhee and Ibn Maajah and declared *hasan* by Shaikh al-Albaanee.

3. The proof for this is that which is authentically reported from Prophet (ﷺ) regarding the major and minor signs of the Hour.

94 Know that the Messenger of Allaah (ﷺ) said, *"My Ummah will split up into seventy three sects, all of them in the Fire except one and it is al-Jamaa'ah." It was said 'Who are they, O Messenger of Allaah?' He replied, "That which I and my Companions are upon today."*[1]

The Religion was a single *Jamaa'ah* up to the time of the *Khilaafah* of 'Umar ibn al-Khattaab and also in the time of 'Uthmaan, *radiallaahu 'anhu*. When he was killed, schism and innovations appeared. People split into parties and sects. Amongst the people were some who remained firm upon the truth. When the affairs worsened, they spoke the truth, acted upon it and called the people to it.

The affairs remained in order until the fourth generation in the *Khilaafah* of so and so. When times changed and people deteriorated greatly, innovations became widespread and there arose many callers inviting away from the way of truth and the *Jamaa'ah*. People were tried with things, which neither the Messenger of Allaah (ﷺ) nor any of his Companions spoke about. People called to sectarianism, whereas the Messenger of Allaah (ﷺ) had forbidden sectarianism. Each group declared the others to be unbelievers. Everyone called to his own opinion and declared those who differed with him to be unbelievers. The ignorant, the common folk and those without knowledge went astray. They caused the people to be greedy for things of this world and to fear worldly punishment; so people followed them out of fear for their worldly affairs and out of desire for this world. So the *Sunnah* and the people of *Sunnah* were suppressed. Innovation appeared and

---

1. The *hadeeth* is *hasan* and is reported by at-Tirmidhee (no. 2643), Ibn Waddaah in *al-Bida'h* (p.85), al-Aajurree in ash-*Sharee'ah* (p.15) and in *al-Arba'een*, al-Haakim (1/128-129), Ibn Nasr in as-*Sunnah* (no.62), al-Laalikaa'ee in as-*Sunnah* (no.147), Ibn al-Jawzee in *Talbees Iblees* (p.16) and al-'Uqailee in *ad-Du'afaa'* (2/262) from the *hadeeth* of 'Abdullaah ibn 'Amr.

became widespread. The people committed disbelief in many ways which they were not aware of. They used analogical reasoning and considered the Power of the Lord, His signs, rulings, commands and prohibitions according to their intellect and opinions. Whatever accorded with their intellect they accepted and whatever did not agree with their intellect they rejected. Islaam became a stranger, the *Sunnah* a stranger and the people of *Sunnah* strangers within their own homes.[1]

95 Know that temporary marriage of convenience (*mut'ah*)[2] and marrying a woman merely to make her lawful for her previous husband (*istihlaal*) is forbidden until the Day of Resurrection.[3]

96 To recognise the excellence of Banu Haashim due to their kinship to the Messenger of Allaah (ﷺ). To recognise the excellence of the *Quraish*,[4] the Arabs and branches of the tribe and recognise their station and rights in Islaam.

---

1. Perhaps the author is referring to what happened due to the trials caused by the saying that the Qur'aan was created and the trial of the scholars of the *Sunnah* regarding it. Refer to *ar-Radd 'alal-Jahmiyyah* of ad-Daarimee.

2. Sabrah al-Juhanee, *radiallaahu 'anhu*, reports that the Messenger of Allaah (ﷺ) said, *"I had permitted temporary marriage of women to you. Now, Allaah has forbidden that for you until the Day of Resurrection. If any of you have any of them, he must let her go and not take back anything which he gave her."* Reported by Muslim (Eng. trans. 2/707/no.3255).

3. 'Alee, *radiallaahu 'anhu*, reports that the Messenger of Allaah (ﷺ) said, *"Allaah has cursed the man who marries a woman in order to make her lawful for her first husband and the one for whom she is made lawful."* The *hadeeth* is *saheeh* and is reported by Ahmad, Abu Daawood (Eng. trans. 2/555/no.2071), at-Tirmdhee and an-Nasaa'ee.

4. He (ﷺ) said, *"Allaah chose Kinaah from the descendents of Ismaa'eel, the Quraish from Kinaah, Banu Haashim from the Quraish and chose me from Banu Haashim."* Refer to *Saheeh Muslim* (Eng. trans. 4/1230/no.5653), Ahmad (4/107) and *as-Sunnah* of Ibn Abee 'Aasim (2/632). For further explanation, refer to Ibn Hajr's *Fathul-Baaree* (13/113). This excellence is only for the Muslims amongst them.

The slave belonging to a people is one of them. To recognise the rights of the rest of the people of Islaam. To recognise the excellence of the Ansaar[1] and the advice the Messenger of Allaah (ﷺ) gave regarding them and his family. Do not abuse them but recognise their excellence. Recognise the excellence of his neighbours from the people of al-Madeenah.

97 May Allaah have mercy upon you! Know that the scholars did not cease refuting the saying of the *Jahmiyyah* to the time of the *Khilaafah* of Banul-'Abbaas, when the lowly and despicable spoke in matters affecting the people and attacked the sayings reported from the Messenger of Allaah (ﷺ) and took to using analogy and opinion. They declared those who disagreed with them to be disbelievers, so that the ignorant, unwary and those without knowledge entered into their saying, so they fell into unbelief without knowing. The *Ummah* was ruined in a number of ways, disbelieved in a number of ways, became heretical in a number of ways, went astray in a number of ways and innovated in a number of ways, except for those who remained firm upon the sayings of the Messenger of Allaah (ﷺ), what he was upon and what his Companions were upon, not declaring any of them to be in error, nor overstepping what they were upon. He finds sufficiency in what they sufficed with, he does not turn away from their way and position, he knows that they were upon correct Islaam and correct Faith; so he follows them in his Religion and finds calmness and knows that the Religion lies in following. Those who are meant to be followed are the Companions of the Muhammad (ﷺ).

---

1. He (ﷺ) said, *"The sign of Eemaan is love for the Ansaar and the sign of hypocrisy is hatred of the Ansaar."* Reported by al-Bukhaaree (Eng. trans. 1/21/ no.16). Refer also to *Fadaailus-Sahaabah* of Imaam Ahmad (2/790).

98 Know that whoever says that his recital of the Qur'aan is created is an innovator. Whoever remains silent and will neither say created nor uncreated, he too, is a *Jahmee*. This was the saying of Ahmad ibn Hanbal.[1]

The Messenger of Allaah (ﷺ) said, *"He amongst you who lives long will see great controversy, so beware of newly invented matters because they are misguidance and take to my Sunnah and the Sunnah of the rightly-guided Khulafaa', grasp that with your molar teeth."*[2]

99 Know that the ruin of the *Jahmiyyah* was that they pondered about the Lord, the Mighty and Majestic. They introduced, 'Why?' and 'How?' They abandoned the narrations, used analogy and weighed the Religion according to their opinions, so they openly showed disbelief and its being disbelief is obvious. They declared the rest of the people to be disbelievers and were lead themselves into divesting (Allaah of His attributes).

---

1. As occurs in *as-Sunnah* (1/163-166) of 'Abdullaah ibn Ahmad ibn Hanbal, *Usool as-Sunnah* (point no.2) of Imaam Ahmad and *Sareeh as-Sunnah* (points 30-33) of at-Tabaree.

The saying of the *Salaf* is that the Qur'aan which is written in the *Mushaf*, memorised in the heart and recited upon the tongue is the uncreated Speech of Allaah. However, due to the fact that the human voice and movement of one's tongue are created actions, the innovators innovated the ambiguous statement 'my recitation of the Qur'aan is created.' This saying leads to the previous saying that the Qur'aan itself is created. Therefore, the scholars such as Imaam Ahmad warned against this. Also, refer to *Khalq Af'aalul-'Ibaad* (nos. 217, 540) of al-Bukhaaree.

2. Reported by Abu Daawood (Eng. trans. 3/1294/no.4590), at-Tirmidhee (no.2678), Ibn Maajah (no.420) and Ahmad in his *Musnad* (4/126) and the *hadeeth* is *saheeh*.

100 Some of the scholars, amongst them Ahmad ibn Hanbal, *radiallaahu 'anhu*, declared the *Jahmee* to be a disbeliever and not from the people of the *Qiblah*. His blood is lawful. He does not inherit, neither is inheritance received from him, since he says that there is no *Jumu'ah* or congregational Prayer, no *'Eid* Prayer, no charity (*Sadaqah*) and because they say, 'one who does not say the Qur'aan is created is a disbeliever.' They allow fighting and killing within the nation of Muhammad (ﷺ). They contradict those who preceded them. They put the people to trial regarding something which neither the Prophet (ﷺ) nor any of his Companions spoke about.

They desire to empty the Mosques and for the congregations to be neglected. They weakened Islaam, caused *Jihaad* to be left and busied themselves with sectarianism. They went against the narrations and spoke up with that which had been abrogated.[1] They used verses of uncertain meaning as clear proof and so caused the people to have doubts about their Religion. They disputed about their Lord and said, 'There is no punishment in the grave, nor any pond (*Hawd*), nor any Intercession and that Paradise and the Fire have not been created.' They rejected much of what the Messenger of Allaah (ﷺ) said. Those who permit the declaration of their being unbelievers declare them to be so and declare the spilling of their blood to be lawful because of these matters. Since, whoever rejects a verse from the Book of Allaah has rejected the whole Book and whoever rejects a *hadeeth* from the Messenger of Allaah (ﷺ) has rejected all of his sayings and is a disbeliever in Allaah, the Sublime.

They continued in time and found rulers who were to assist them in this and who subjected those who refused it to the sword

---

1. The *Mu'tazilah* and the *Raafidah* denied abrogation (*naskh*). Before them, the Jews had denied it.

or the whip. Knowledge of the *Sunnah* and the *Jamaa'ah* was wiped away and weakened by them, so that they became suppressed due to the manifesting of innovation and speech about it and their great number. They established sittings, manifested their opinions, wrote books about them, enticed the people and they sought leadership for them.

It was a very great trial.[1] Only those whom Allaah protected were saved from it. The slightest that a person would be affected by sitting with them was that he would be caused to doubt about his Religion, or to follow them, or to hold their saying to be true, not knowing whether it was the truth or falsehood, so he became one who doubted. So the people were ruined, until the time of Ja'far who was known as al-Mutawakkil,[2] through whom Allaah extinguished innovation and manifested the truth and the people of the *Sunnah*. They spoke out, despite their small number and the great number of innovators, right up to this day.[3] As for their principles and misguidance, some of them have remained acting upon it and calling to it, with none to prevent them from their sayings and actions!

---

1. Proclamation was made that everyone had to adhere to the belief of the Mu'tazilah, that the Qur'aan was created! The scholars were threatened and ordered to agree to this. Those who refused to assent verbally were imprisoned, threatened with death and tortured. Imaam Ahmad, *rahimahullaah*, stood firm, despite months in prison, constantly being brought before those in authority and threatened with death and kept in chains. Eventually, he was lashed severely in public. 'Alee ibn al-Madeenee said, "Indeed, Allaah aided this Religion through Abu Bakr on the day of apostasy (*riddah*) and through Ahmad ibn Hanbal on the day of the trial (*mihnah*)." Reported by adh-Dhahabee in *Tadhkiratul-Huffaadh* (2/432).

2. The 'Abbasid Caliph, al-Mutawakkil 'alallaah: Abul-Fadl, Ja'far son of al-Mu'tasimbillaah, al-Qurashee. He died in the year 247 after the Hijrah. May the Mercy of Allaah be upon him.

3. Refer to the letter of Ahmad ibn Hanbal to al-Mutawakkil, mentioned in *as-Sunnah* of his son 'Abdullaah as point number 84.

71

101 Know that there has never been any heresy except from the ignorant rabble who follow anyone who calls out wildly. They bend with every wind that blows, so anyone who is like that has no Religion. Allaah, the Blessed and Most High, says:

فَمَا ٱخْتَلَفُوٓا۟ إِلَّا مِنۢ بَعْدِ مَا جَآءَهُمُ ٱلْعِلْمُ بَغْيًۢا بَيْنَهُمْ

They did not differ until after the knowledge came to them, through envy among themselves.[1]

وَمَا ٱخْتَلَفَ فِيهِ إِلَّا ٱلَّذِينَ أُوتُوهُ مِنۢ بَعْدِ مَا جَآءَتْهُمُ ٱلْبَيِّنَـٰتُ بَغْيًۢا بَيْنَهُمْ

Only those to whom (the Scripture) was given differed concerning it after clear Proofs had come to them through hatred one to another.[2]

They are the evil scholars, those greedy (for this world) and who are the innovators.

102 Know that there will not cease to be a group of the people of the truth and the *Sunnah* amongst the people, whom Allaah will guide and through them guide others and revive the *Sunnah* through them. They are the ones whom Allaah, the Most High, describes, those who are few in the time of controversy. He says:

وَمَا ٱخْتَلَفَ فِيهِ إِلَّا ٱلَّذِينَ أُوتُوهُ مِنۢ بَعْدِ مَا جَآءَتْهُمُ ٱلْبَيِّنَـٰتُ بَغْيًۢا بَيْنَهُمْ

Only those to whom (the Scripture) was given differed concerning it after clear Proofs had come to them through hatred one to another.[3]

---

1. Soorah al-Jaathiyah (45):17
2. Soorah al-Baqarah (2):213
3. Soorah al-Baqarah (2):213

He excepted these people, saying:

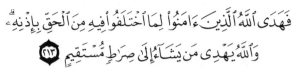

فَهَدَى ٱللَّهُ ٱلَّذِينَ ءَامَنُوا لِمَا ٱخْتَلَفُوا فِيهِ مِنَ ٱلْحَقِّ بِإِذْنِهِ ۗ
وَٱللَّهُ يَهْدِى مَن يَشَاءُ إِلَىٰ صِرَٰطٍ مُّسْتَقِيمٍ ۝

Then Allaah by His leave guided those who believed in the truth, concerning that wherein they differed. For Allaah guides whom He wills to a straight path.[1]

The Messenger of Allaah (ﷺ) said, *"There will not cease to be a group of my Ummah, uppermost upon the truth. They will not be harmed by those who forsake them, until Allaah's affair comes to pass and they are uppermost."*[2]

103 May Allaah have mercy upon you! Know that knowledge is not in merely narrating a great deal and (having many) books. The scholar is the one who follows the Book and the *Sunnah*, even if his knowledge is limited[3] and he has only a few books. Whoever conflicts with the Book and the *Sunnah* is an innovator, even if he narrates much and has many books.

---

1. Soorah al-Baqarah (2):213
2. Reported by Muslim (Eng. trans. 3/1061/no.4715), at-Tirmidhee (no. 2230) and Ibn Maajah (no. 10). Also, refer to *Saheeh al-Bukhaaree* (Eng. trans. 9/309-310/nos.414-415) and *Saheeh Muslim* (Eng. trans. 3/1061-1062/nos.4716-4722).
   The Prophet (ﷺ) said, *"This Knowledge will be carried by the trustworthy ones of every generation. They will expel from it the alterations made by those going beyond bounds, the false claims of the liars and the false interpretations of the ignorant."* Reported by Ibn 'Adiyy, Ibn 'Asaakir and others and is *saheeh*.
3. Ash-Shaafi'ee, *rahimahullaah,* said, "Knowledge is not what is memorised, but what benefits." Reported in *Hilyatul-Awliyaa'* of Abu Nu'aym (9/123).

104 May Allaah have mercy upon you! Know that whoever speaks about the Religion of Allaah from his opinion, analogy and interpretation, without proof from the *Sunnah* and the *Jamaa'ah* has spoken about Allaah that which he does not know.[1] Whoever says about Allaah what he does not know is one who has overstepped the bounds.[2]

---

1. In the Book of Allaah, speaking about Allaah without knowledge is shown to be a form of *Shirk*. He, the One free of all defects, says:

قُلْ إِنَّمَا حَرَّمَ رَبِّيَ ٱلْفَوَٰحِشَ مَا ظَهَرَ مِنْهَا وَمَا بَطَنَ وَٱلْإِثْمَ وَٱلْبَغْىَ بِغَيْرِ ٱلْحَقِّ وَأَن تُشْرِكُوا۟ بِٱللَّهِ مَا لَمْ يُنَزِّلْ بِهِۦ سُلْطَٰنًا وَأَن تَقُولُوا۟ عَلَى ٱللَّهِ مَا لَا تَعْلَمُونَ ٣٣

Say: The things that my Lord has forbidden are: Shameful deeds, whether open or secret, sins (of all kinds), assigning of partners to Allaah, for which He had given no authority and saying things about Allaah of which you have no knowledge.

Soorah al-A'raaf (7):33

2. Masrooq, *rahimahullaah*, said: We entered upon 'Abdullaah ibn Mas'ood and he said, "O people ! Whoever knows something then let him speak according to it. Whoever does not know, let him say, 'Allaah knows best,' since this too, is from knowledge, that you say concerning that which you do not know, 'Allaah knows best.' Allaah, the Mighty and Majestic, said to His Prophet (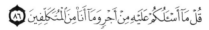):

قُلْ مَا أَسْـَٔلُكُمْ عَلَيْهِ مِنْ أَجْرٍ وَمَا أَنَا۠ مِنَ ٱلْمُتَكَلِّفِينَ ٨٦

Say: No reward do I ask of you for this (Qur'aan). Nor am I a pretender."

Soorah Saad (38):86

Reported by al-Bukhaaree (Eng. trans. 6/314/no.333).

105   The truth is that which comes from Allaah, the Mighty and Majestic. The *Sunnah* is that which the Messenger of Allaah (ﷺ) laid down and the *Jamaa'ah* is that which the Companions of the Messenger of Allaah (ﷺ) were united upon in the *Khilaafah* of Abu Bakr, 'Umar and 'Uthmaan.

106   He who limits himself to the *Sunnah* of the Messenger of Allaah (ﷺ) and that which his Companions and the *Jamaa'ah* were upon is successful and triumphs over all the people of innovation and is saved and his Religion is preserved, if Allaah wills. Since, the Messenger of Allaah (ﷺ) said, *"My Ummah will split .."* and the Messenger of Allaah (ﷺ) told us that which would be the saved sect from them saying, *"That which I and my Companions are upon."*[1] This is the cure, the explanation, the clear affair and the straight and distinct road. The Messenger of Allaah (ﷺ) said, *"Beware of going to extremes and harshness. Beware of exaggeration and cling to the ancient Religion."*[2]

---

1. Reported by at-Tirmidhee (no. 2643) and others and is *hasan* as has preceded.

2. This is not a *hadeeth* of the Prophet (ﷺ), but is a saying of Ibn Mas'ood, *radiallaahu 'anhu,* as reported by ad-Daarimee in his *Sunan* (1/50/ nos. 144, 145), 'Abdur-Razzaaq in his *Musannaf* (10/252) and Ibn Nasr in *as-Sunnah* (no.85) and others and is *saheeh* as such.

Ibn 'Abbaas, *radiallaahu 'anhu,* reports that the Prophet (ﷺ) said, *"Beware of exaggeration in the Religion, for indeed, those before you were destroyed due to exaggeration in the Religion."* Reported by Ahmad, an-Nasaa'ee and Ibn Maajah and is *saheeh.*

Ibn Mas'ood, *radiallaahu 'anhu,* reports that the Prophet (ﷺ) said, *"Those who go to extremes are destroyed."* Reported by Ahmad, Muslim and Abu Daawood (Eng. trans. 3/1294/no.4591) and is *saheeh.*

107   Know that the ancient Religion is how it was from the death of the Messenger of Allaah (ﷺ) till the death of 'Uthmaan ibn 'Affaan, *radiallaahu 'anhu*. His murder was the beginning of sectarian dissension and the start of disagreements. So the *Ummah* fought among themselves, split, followed greed and desires and inclined towards this world. There is no permit for anyone to do anything which has been introduced, which the Companions of the Allaah's Messenger (ﷺ) were not upon, nor for any man to call to anything innovated before him by people of innovation, he would then be just like the one who innovated it. So anyone who claims that, or speaks according to it, has rejected the *Sunnah*, opposed the truth and the *Jamaa'ah* and has made innovations lawful. He is more harmful to the *Ummah* than Iblees.[1]

108   Whoever realises what the innovators have abandoned of the *Sunnah* and left behind and he clings to it, he is a person of the *Sunnah* and the *Jamaa'ah*. He should be followed, helped and protected. He is one of those whom the Prophet (ﷺ) bequeathed should be looked after.

109   May Allaah have mercy upon you! Know that the roots of innovation are four. From these, seventy two innovations branch off, each of these have offshoots, so that they amount to two thousand eight hundred. All of them are misguidance. All of them are in the Fire except for one, which is those who believe in that contained in this book, believing in it firmly without having any doubt or uncertainty in their heart, such a person is a person of the *Sunnah* and one who is saved, if Allaah wills.[2]

---

1. Al-Laalikaa'ee reports in *as-Sunnah* (no.238) that Sufyaan ath-Thawree said, "Innovation is more beloved to Iblees than sin. A sin may be repented from, but innovation is not repented from."

2. i.e. whatever the book comprises of, from the Sayings of Allaah, the words of His Prophet (ﷺ) and that which the Companions were united upon.

110   May Allaah have mercy upon you! Know that if the people were to desist from newly introduced matters, not entering into any of them at all and did not say anything for which there was no narration from the Messenger of Allaah (صلى الله عليه وسلم) or from his Companions, there would not be any innovation.

111   May Allaah have mercy upon you! Know that there is nothing between a servant and his being a Believer or becoming an unbeliever, except that he denies something which Allaah, the Most High, has sent down, or adds, or takes away anything from the Speech of Allaah, or denies anything which Allaah, the Mighty and Majestic, said, or denies anything said by the Messenger of Allaah (صلى الله عليه وسلم), so fear Allaah. May Allaah have mercy upon you! Beware for your own soul and beware of going into exaggeration in the Religion because it is not from the way of truth at all.

112   Everything that I have described to you in this book is from Allaah, the Most High, from the Messenger of Allaah (صلى الله عليه وسلم), from his Companions, from the *Taabi'een* and from the third generation to the fourth. So fear Allaah, O servant of Allaah! Affirm, submit, surrender to and be pleased with what is in this book. Do not hide this book from anyone of the people of the *Qiblah*. Perhaps through it, Allaah will bring a confused person out of his confusion, or an innovator out of his innovation or a misguided one out of his misguidance and he may be saved through it. So fear Allaah and take to the affair as it originally was. That is what I have described to you in this book. May Allaah have mercy upon a person, and his parents, who reads this book, circulates it, acts upon it, calls to it and uses it as a proof, for it is the Religion of Allaah[1] and Allaah's

---

1. The Religion of Allaah as is well-known is the Book of Allaah and the *Sunnah* of His Messenger (صلى الله عليه وسلم) as understood by the Pious Predecessors. As for the speech of people, everyone is correct in some things and incorrect in others, except for the Prophet (صلى الله عليه وسلم).

Messenger (ﷺ). Whoever allows something contrary to this book, he is not practising Allaah's Religion and has refused all of it, just as if a servant believed all that Allaah, the Blessed and Most High, says, except that he doubted about a single letter, then he has rejected everything which Allaah said and is an unbeliever, just as the testification that 'none has the right to be worshipped except Allaah' is not accepted from a person unless his intention is pure and sincere and he has full certainty. Likewise, Allaah will not accept anything from the *Sunnah* from one who abandons a part of it. Whoever contradicts and rejects anything from the *Sunnah* has rejected all of the *Sunnah*. Accept and avoid contending and disputing, it is not from Allaah's Religion, at all. Your time, in particular, is a time of evil, so beware of Allaah.

113   When turmoil (*fitnah*) occurs then remain within your house[1] and flee from the neighbourhood of tumult. Beware of blind following and every case of fighting between Muslims, for this world is discord and a trial. Fear Allaah, who is Alone having no partner. Do not go out in it, do not fight in it, do not take part in it, do not take sides in it, nor incline towards either (side) and do not have love for any of their affairs, since it is said, 'he who loves the deeds of a people, good or bad, is just like the one who commits them.' May Allaah grant us and you those things pleasing to Him and keep us away from disobedience to Him.

---

1. Ibn az-Zubayr narrates: *My close friend, Abul-Qaasim* (ﷺ)*advised me, "If you reach anything of the tumult, go to Uhud and blunt your sword upon it, then remain in your house."* Reported by Ahmad in *al-Musnad* (4/226 and 5/69). Its *isnaad* is *hasan*, as has been mentioned by Shaikh al-Albaanee in *as-Saheehah* (3/no.1373).

114   Look into the stars only sparingly, just enough for you to know the times of Prayer. Turn away from other than that, since it leads to apostasy.[1]

115   Beware of looking into theological rhetoric and sitting with the people of theological rhetoric.[2]

116   Stick to the narrations and the people of narrations, ask them, sit with them and take from them.

117   Know that Allaah has not been worshipped with the like of fear of Allaah; the way of fear, sadness, having apprehension and feeling shy before Allaah, the Blessed and Most High.

118   Beware of sitting with those who call to passion and love and seclude themselves with women and sit where they pass because they are all upon error.[3]

---

1. The Messenger of Allaah (ﷺ) said, *"When my Companions are mentioned, withhold. When the stars are mentioned, withhold and when Pre-decree is mentioned, withhold."* Reported by at-Tabaraanee in *al-Kabeer*. Shaikh al-Albaanee has declared it *saheeh* in *Saheeh al-Jaami'* (no.545).

2. It is reported that Imaam ash-Shaafi'ee, *rahimahullaah,* said, "My ruling regarding the people of theological rhetoric is that they should be beaten with palm branches and shoes and led round the markets and it be said: This is the punishment of those who have abandoned the Book and the *Sunnah* and taken to theological rhetoric." Reported by al-Baghawee in *Sharh as-Sunnah* (1/218).

   Imaam Ahmad, *rahimahullaah,* said, "A person of theological rhetoric will never succeed. The scholars of theological rhetoric are wicked heretics." Reported by Ibn al-Jawzee in *Manaaqib Ahmad* (p.204).

3. Like many of the sects of the misguided Soofees.

119 May Allaah have mercy upon you! Know that Allaah, the Blessed and Most High, called all of creation to worship Him. (He) blessed whomsoever He wished with Islaam, by His grace.[1]

120 Remain quiet about the fighting between 'Alee and Mu'aawiyah and 'Aaishah, Talhah and az-Zubayr. May Allaah have mercy upon them all and upon those with them. Do not dispute about them, leave their affair to Allaah, the blessed and Most High, since the Messenger of Allaah (ﷺ) said, *"Beware of speaking about my Companions and in-laws"*[2] and he (ﷺ) said, *"Indeed Allaah, the Most High, looked upon the people of Badr and said: Do what you wish for I have forgiven you."*[3]

---

1. He, the Most High, says:

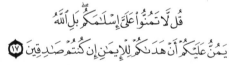

Say: Count not your Islaam as a favour upon me: No! Allaah has conferred a favour upon you, that He has guided you to Faith, if you are indeed true.

Soorah al-Hujuraat (49):17

2. The *hadeeth* with this wording is not authentic. However, what is authentic is the *hadeeth* of Abu Sa'eed, *radiallaahu 'anhu*, who reports that the Prophet (ﷺ) said, *"Do not abuse my Companions, for if any of you were to spend gold equal to Uhud in charity, it would not equal a handful of one of them or even half of that."* Reported by al-Bukhaaree (Eng. trans. 5/17/no.22) and Muslim (Eng. trans. 4/1349/no.6168).

3. Reported by al-Bukhaaree (Eng. trans. 5/212-214/no.318) and Muslim (Eng. trans. 4/1331/no.6087).

121 May Allaah have mercy upon you! Know that the wealth of a Muslim is unlawful except what he gives willingly.[1] If a man has some wealth that was attained illegally, it is his concern. It is not permissible to take any of it from him, except with his permission. Perhaps he will repent and wish to restore it to its rightful owner but you will have taken something unlawful.

122 Means of earning which are clear to you to be correct are unrestricted, except for that which is found to be corrupt. If it is corrupt, he takes from it what is sufficient to support himself and (he) does not say, 'I will abandon earning and take what people will give me.' This was not done by the Companions, nor by the scholars up to this time of ours. 'Umar ibn al-Khattaab, *radiallaahu 'anhu*, said, "Earning of which a part is impure is better than having need of the people."[2]

123 The five daily Prayers must be prayed behind anyone except a *Jahmee,* since he denies (all of the attributes of Allaah). If you have prayed behind him, repeat your Prayer. On the day of *Jumu'ah,* if your *Imaam* is a *Jahmee* and he is a ruler, pray behind him, (but) repeat your Prayer.[3] If your *Imaam,* whether a ruler or not, is a person of the *Sunnah*, pray behind him and do not repeat your Prayer.

---

1. The Messenger of Allaah (ﷺ) said, *"The wealth of a Muslim is not permissible except what he gives willingly."* Reported by Ahmad and declared *saheeh* by Shaikh al-Albaanee in *Saheehul-Jaami'* (no. 7539) and *al-Irwaa'* (no. 1459).

2. Reported by Wakee' ibn al-Jarrah, as occurs in *Kanzul-'Ummaal* (4/ 122) and by Ibn al-Jawzee in *Manaaqib 'Umar* (p.194).

3. This is reported by 'Abdullaah ibn Ahmad, as the saying of his father, Imaam Ahmad, in *as-Sunnah* (nos.4-5).

124   To have Faith that Abu Bakr and 'Umar, *rahmatullaahi 'alaihimaa*, are within the room of 'Aaishah along with the Messenger of Allaah (ﷺ). They were buried there with him. If you come to their graves, you must give *salaam* to them after Allaah's Messenger (ﷺ).[1]

125   Ordering good and forbidding the evil is an obligation,[2] except if you fear the sword or rod of a person.

126   Greetings of *salaam* are to be given to all of Allaah's worshippers.

127   Whoever abandons the *Jumu'ah* or congregational Prayer in the mosque, without an excuse is an innovator.[3] An excuse may be illness, because of which one is unable to go out to the mosque, or fear of an oppressive ruler and what is besides that is not an excuse.

128 Whoever prays behind an Imaam and does not follow him, there is no Prayer for him.[4]

---

1. i.e. one gives greetings of *salaam* to them, just as one does when visiting the graves of the Muslims.

2. The one ordering the good and forbidding the evil must have the required knowledge, otherwise he may cause more harm than good and he will only succeed in causing a greater evil, which is forbidden.

3. Congregational Prayer in the mosque is an obligation upon the sane, adult males, who able to attend. This is the most correct saying of the scholars. Refer to *Prayer in Congregation* by 'Abdullaah as-Sabt.

4. The Prophet (ﷺ) said, *"The Imaam is appointed to be followed; when he says takbeer, say takbeer; when he prostrates, you should prostrate; when he rises up, you should rise up and when he says 'Allaah listens to the one who praises Him,' say 'Our Lord! All praise is for You.' When he prays sitting, all of you should pray sitting."* Reported by al-Bukhaaree and Muslim (Eng. trans. 1/226/no.817).

129 Ordering good and forbidding evil are to be done with the hand,[1] the tongue and the heart, not with the sword.[2]

130 The blameless Muslim is one who does not show signs of anything suspicious.

131 Everything (some) worshippers claim as hidden knowledge (*'Ilmul-Baatin*), which is not found in the Book and the *Sunnah,* is innovation and misguidance. It is not to be acted upon nor called to.[3]

132 A woman, who gives herself in marriage to a man, is not lawful for him. They are both to be punished if he has violated her, unless it is performed with a guardian, two just witnesses and a dower.[4]

---

1. The Messenger of Allaah (ﷺ) said, *"He amongst you who sees evil, let him change it with his hand. If he is unable, then with his tongue and if he is unable, then with his heart - and that is the weakest of Faith."* Reported by Ahmad, Muslim (Eng. trans. 1/33/no.77), Abu Daawood, at-Tirmidhee and Ibn Maajah.

2. Ibn Rajab says in *Jaami' ul-'Uloom wal-Hikam* (p.304), "Changing with the hand does not mean fighting. This is also stated by Ahmad, in the narration of Saalih, he said, 'Changing with the hand does not mean with the sword and the use of weapons.'" So, the use of the sword is not for the public, rather it is for the ruler. This saying of Imaam Ahmad is also reported by Ibn Muflih in *al-Aadaabush-Shar'iyyah* (1/163).

3. This is what the extreme innovators, amongst them the *Baatinees* and extreme *Soofees,* call to. They explain things away by claiming that they have an outer aspect and an inner aspect. They twist the Book of Allaah and His *Sharee'ah* to suit their own desires. Their claim of receiving hidden religious knowledge, outside of the Book and the *Sunnah,* is disbelief.

4. The Messenger of Allaah (ﷺ) said, *"There is no marriage without a guardian."* Reported by Ahmad, Abu Daawood (Eng. trans. 2/558/no.2080) and at-Tirmidhee.

Ibn 'Abbaas, *radiallaaahu 'anhummaa,* said, "There is no marriage except with a guardian advising and two just witnesses." Reported by al-Baihaqee, ash-Shaafi'ee in his *Musnad* and al-Baghawee in *Sharh us-Sunnah* (9/45).

133   If you see a man criticising the Companions of the Messenger of Allaah (ﷺ), know that he is a person of wicked speech and desires, since the Messenger of Allaah (ﷺ) said, *"When my Companions are mentioned then withhold."*[1] The Prophet (ﷺ) knew of any slips they would make after his death, yet still he did not speak about them except good. He also said, *"Leave my Companions and do not speak about them except good."*[2] Do not discuss about their slips or wars, nor that of which you have no knowledge. Do not listen to (such talk) from anyone, for if you do, your heart will not remain safe and sound.[3]

134   If you hear someone criticising or rejecting the narrations or desiring something other than the narrations, have doubt about his Islaam. Do not doubt about his being a person of desires and innovation.

---

1. Refer to point 28 and its accompanying footnote.

The Prophet (ﷺ) said, *"Whoever abuses my Companions, upon them is the curse of Allaah, the angels and all the people."* Reported by at-Tabaraanee from Ibn 'Abbaas and Ibn 'Umar. Al-Albaanee declares the *hadeeth hasan* in *as-Saheehah* (no.2340).

Al-Laalikaa'ee reports in *as-Sunnah* (no.2359) that Imaam Ahmad said, "If you see anyone speaking ill of the Companions of the Messenger of Allaah (ﷺ), doubt his Islaam."

2. The wording as reported by Imaam Ahmad is, *"Leave my Companions for me. For by Him in whose Hand is my soul! If you were to spend the like of Uhud or the mountains, in gold, you would not reach their actions."* Declared *saheeh* by Shaikh al-Albaanee in *Saheehul-Jaami'* (no. 3380).

3. We should also hate those who have any ill-feeling against any of the Companions, since Allaah, the Most High, declared that He is pleased with them. Refer to Soorah al-Hashr, *Aayaat* 8-10, Soorah at-Tawbah, *Aayah* 100 and Soorah al-Fath, *Aayah* 18. Indeed, those who attack the Companions are wicked heretics seeking to destroy Islaam, since the whole Religion was transmitted to us by the Companions.

135   Know that a ruler's oppression does not reduce or remove anything which Allaah has made obligatory upon the tongue of the Messenger (ﷺ). His oppression is upon himself. Your acts of obedience and good deeds along with behaving well towards him are complete, if Allaah, the Most High, wills. Accompany them in all acts of obedience such as the congregational and *Jumu'ah* Prayers, for you have your independent intention in that.[1]

136   If you find a man making supplication against the ruler, know that he is a person of innovation. If you find a person making supplication for the ruler to be upright, know that he is a person of the *Sunnah*, if Allaah wills. Fudayl ibn 'Iyaad[2] said, "If I had an invocation which was to be answered, I would not make it except for the ruler." It was said to him, "O Abu 'Alee, explain that to us," he replied, "If I made an invocation for myself, it would not go beyond me. Whereas if I make it for the ruler, he is corrected and through that, the servants and the land are set in order."[3]

---

1. Shaikh ul-Islaam Ibn Taimiyyah, *rahimahullaah*, says in *Majmoo' al-Fataawaa* (22/61), "The rulers are not to be fought due to committing sins. Even though a person may be killed for some sins, such as adultery and the like. However, it is not permitted to fight the rulers for doing things for which a person may be killed, since the corruption caused by this fighting is far greater than the corruption of a major sin committed by the ruler."
2. Al-Fudayl ibn 'Iyaad ibn Mas'ood, Shaikh ul-Islaam, Abu 'Alee, al-Yarboo'ee, al-Khursaanee. He was born in Samarqand and grew up to be a highway robber. However, his heart was moved upon hearing the Qur'aan recited and he repented and then travelled in search of knowledge to Koofah, eventually settling in Makkah. Some of his students were Ibn al-Mubaarak, Yahyaa al-Qattaan, 'Abdur-Rahmaan ibn Mahdee, 'Abdur-Razzaq, ash-Shaafi'ee and Qutaibah ibn Sa'eed. Ibn al-Mubaarak said, "No one better than Fudayl ibn 'Iyyaad remains upon the face of the earth." Haaroon ar-Rasheed said, "I have not seen any scholar with greater dignity than Maalik, nor anyone more pious than al-Fudayl." *As-Siyar* (8/421-441) and *Tadhkiratul-Huffaadh* (1/245-246) of adh-Dhahabee.
2. This narration is reported by Abu Nu'aym in *al-Hilyah* (8/91) with a *saheeh isnaad* and by al-Khallaal in *as-Sunnah* (no.9).

We are ordered to make supplication for them (i.e. the rulers) to be upright. We have not been ordered to make supplication against them, even if they commit tyranny and oppression, since their tyranny and oppression reflect only upon themselves but their rectitude is good for themselves and the Muslims.

137 We do not say anything except good about the 'Mothers of the Believers.'[1]

138 If you see a man constant in performing the Obligatory Prayers in congregation, with the ruler or other than him, know that he is a person of the *Sunnah*, if Allaah wills. If you see a man neglecting the Obligatory Prayers in congregation, even with the ruler, know that he is a person of innovation.

139 The lawful is that which you would witness and swear to be lawful. Likewise the prohibited. That which causes uneasiness in the heart is something doubtful.[2]

140 The blameless one is he whose blamelessness is apparent and the dishonourable is the one exposed as such.

---

1. This is the term of respect used for all the wives of the Prophet (ﷺ). This is how they have been termed in Soorah al-Ahzaab, Aayah number 6.
2. An-Nu'maan ibn Basheer said: I heard Allaah's Messenger (ﷺ) say, *"That which is lawful is clear and that which is forbidden is clear. Between these two are doubtful matters..."* Reported by al-Bukhaaree (Eng. trans. 1/44/no.49) and Muslim (Eng. trans. 3/840/no.3882).

141   If you hear a man saying, 'So and so is a *Mushabbih*' or that, 'So and so speaks with *tashbeeh*', then suspect the one saying so and know that he is a *Jahmee*. If you hear a man saying, 'So and so is a *Naasibee*,' know that the one saying so is a *Raafidee*. If you hear a man saying, 'Tell me about *Tawheed*' and 'Explain *Tawheed* to me,' know that he is a *Khaarijee*, a *Mu'tazilee*.[1] (If you hear a man) saying, 'So and so is a *Mujbir (Jabariyy)*,' or, 'He speaks with *Ijbaar*,' or he speaks about 'Justice,' ('*Adl*) know that he is a *Qadariyy*. Since these names are a novelty introduced by the innovators.[2]

---

1. What the author means here by *Tawheed* is the *Tawheed* claimed by the *Mu'tazilah* as one of their five principles, that is the denial of Allaah's attributes, i.e. something contrary to true *Tawheed*.

2. The author indicates how the extreme innovators accuse the people of the *Sunnah*, those who do not share their deviation, but take the middle path. So when they, for example, give due love and respect to the Companions, they are accused by the *Raafidees* of having less love for 'Alee, *radiallaahu 'anhu*, than is due and indeed of hating him and the family of the Prophet (ﷺ) (*Ahlul-Bait*) and of being *Naasibees*. Whereas the *Naasibees* would accuse them of being *Raafidees* and so on with the rest of the misguided sects.

Imaam Abu Haatim ar-Raazee, *rahimahullaah*, said, "The sign of the people of innovation is that they attack those who cling to the narrations. The sign of the heretical apostates is that they call *Ahl us-Sunnah* 'The worthless ones' intending thereby to annul the narrations. The sign of the *Jahmiyyah* is that they call *Ahl us-Sunnah* '*Mushabbihah*' (those who declare Allaah to be like the creation). The sign of the *Qadariyyah* is that they call *Ahl us-Sunnah* '*Jabariyyah*.' The sign of the *Murji'ah* is that they call *Ahl us-Sunnah* 'antagonists and claimants of deficiency.' The sign of the *Raafidees* is that they call *Ahl us-Sunnah* '*Naasibees*.' *Ahl us-Sunnah* do not have but one name." (*Ahl us-Sunnah* (pp.21-22) of Abu Haatim ar-Raazee and Abu Zur'atur-Raazee, checked by Saalih ibn 'Uthmaan al-Lahhaam and *as-Sunnah* (p.179) of al-Laalikaa'ee with a *saheeh isnaad*).

Refer to appendix 3 (pp.116-117) for a brief explanation of the beliefs of these innovated sects.

142 'Abdullaah ibn al-Mubaarak said, "Do not take anything from the view of the *Raafidees* from the people of Koofah. Do not take anything about the use of the sword from the people of Shaam (Palestine and Syria), nor about Divine Pre-decree (*Qadr*) from the people of Basrah, nor concerning *'Irjaa* from the people of Khuraasaan, nor from the people of Makkah concerning money changing, nor from the people of Madeenah concerning singing, do not take any of these from them."[1]

143 If you find a man who loves Abu Hurairah,[2] Anas ibn Maalik[3] and Usayd ibn Hudayr,[4] know that he is a person of the

---

1. What Ibn al-Mubaarak, *rahimahullaah,* means here is to avoid choosing the mistaken allowances made by different scholars, in different areas - since the one who does so is playing with Religion.

2. Abu Hurairah, 'Abdur-Rahmaan ibn Sakhr ad-Dawsee. He came as a *muhaajir* to the Prophet (ﷺ) at the time of Khaybar. He memorised the greatest number of *ahaadeeth* of the Prophet (ﷺ). Over eight hundred people have narrated from him. He died in the year 58H, *radiallaahu 'anhu.*

The Prophet (ﷺ) supplicated for him and his mother, saying, *"O Allaah! Make these servants of Your's beloved to the Believers and make the Believers beloved to them."* Reported by Muslim (Eng. trans. 4/1329/no.6082).

3. Anas ibn Maalik ibn an-Nadr, Abu Hamzah, al-Ansaaree, an-Najjaaree. He was the servant of the Prophet (ﷺ), whom he stayed closely attached to for ten years from when he migrated until the death of Prophet (ﷺ). He himself was one of the last Companions to die. He died in 93H in Basrah, at the age of 103.

Allaah's Messenger (ﷺ) supplicated for him, saying, *"O Allaah! Grant him increase in wealth and children and bless him in what You bestow upon him."* Reported by Muslim (Eng. trans. 4/1322/no.6059). In another narration, Anas added, "By Allaah! My fortune is now huge. My children and grandchildren exceed one hundred in number." (*Saheeh Muslim* no.6063)

4. Usayd ibn Hudayr ibn Simaak al-Ansaaree, al-Ashhalee, Abu Yahyaa. He was one of those who gave the pledge at 'Aqabah. He was wounded seven times during the Battle of Uhud. He died in 20H and was buried in al-Baqee'.

Allaah's Messenger (ﷺ) said, *"What an excellent man is Abu Bakr! What an excellent man is 'Umar! What an excellent man is Usayd ibn Hudayr! What an excellent man is Thaabit ibn Qays ibn Shimaas! What an excellent man is Mu'aadh ibn Jabal! What an excellent man is Mu'aadh ibn 'Amr ibn al-Jamooh."* Reported by at-Tirmidhee (no.4064) and is *saheeh.*

Sunnah, if Allaah wills. If you see a man loving Ayyoob,[1] Ibn 'Awn,[2] Yunus ibn 'Ubaid,[3] 'Abdullaah ibn Idrees al-Awdee,[4] ash-Sha'bee,[5] Maalik ibn Mighwal,[6] Yazeed ibn Zurai',[7] Mu'aadh ibn

---

1. Ayyoob ibn Kaisaan as-Sakhtiyaanee, Abu Bakr, al-Basree. He was a firm, reliable scholar and narrator and worshipper from the period of the *taabi'een*. He died in 131H. Shu'bah said, "I did not see the like of him. He was the noblest of the scholars." Refer to *Hilyatul-Awliyaa* (3/2) and *Siyar A'laamin-Nubalaa* (6/15).

2. 'Abdullaah ibn 'Awn, Abu 'Awn, al-Muzanee. He was a reliable and noble contemporary of Ayyoob. He was from Basrah and died in 150 H. Qurrah said, "We used to be amazed by the piety of Ibn Seereen, then we forgot him due to Ibn 'Awn." Refer to *Siyar A'laamin-Nubalaa* (6/364).

3. Yoonus ibn 'Ubaid ibn Deenaar al-'Abdee, a noble and pious narrator. He was from Basrah and died in 139H. Sa'eed ibn 'Aamir said, "I never saw a man more excellent than Yoonus ibn 'Ubaid. The people of Basrah are of the same opinion." Refer to *Siyar A'laamin-Nubalaa* (6/288).

4. 'Abdullaah ibn Idrees al-Awdee was one of the great scholars and was an exemplary Imaam. Ahmad ibn Hanbal said regarding him, "He was unique and firmly upon the *Sunnah*." Refer to *Taareekh Baghdaad* (9/415), *Tadhkiratul-Huffaadh* (1/282), *at-Tahdheeb* (5/144) and *Siyar A'laamin-Nubalaa* (9/42).

5. 'Aamir ibn Sharaaheel ash-Sha'bee, Abu 'Amr al-Hamdaanee. He was the exemplary *Imaam* and follower of the *Sunnah*. Makhool said, "I have not seen anyone more knowledgeable than ash-Sha'bee." He died in 103H.

6. Maalik ibn Mighwaal, Abu 'Abdullaah. He was the trustworthy scholar of Koofah. He died in 159 H. Al-'Ijlee said, "A righteous man, foremost in excellence." Refer to *at-Tahdheeb* (10/22) and *Siyar A'laamin-Nubalaa* (7/174).

7. Yazeed ibn Zurai', Abu Mu'aawiyah. Ahmad ibn Hanbal said, "He was the sweet-smelling flower of al-Basrah, extremely precise and fully competent in memorising." He died in 182 H. Refer to *at-Tahdheeb* (11/325) and *Siyar A'laamin-Nubalaa* (8/296).

Mu'aadh,[1] Wahb ibn Jareer,[2] Hammaad ibn Zayd,[3] Hammaad ibn Salamah,[4] Maalik ibn Anas,[5] al-Awzaa'ee[6] and Zaaidah ibn Qudaamah,[7] know that he is a person of the *Sunnah*.

---

1. Mu'aadh ibn Mu'aadh ibn Nasr al-'Anbaree, Abul-Muthannaa. He was a scholar and judge of Basrah. Imaam Ahmad said concerning him, "He reached the highest degree of precision and reliability in Basrah and he is a coolness for the eyes in *hadeeth*." He died in 196 H. Refer to *Siyaar A'laamin-Nubalaa* (9/54) and *at-Tahdheeb* (10/194).

2. Wahb ibn Jareer al-Azdee, Abul-'Abbaas. He was from Basrah and died in 206H. Ahmad ibn Hanbal said, "He was never seen with Shu'bah but he was a man of the *Sunnah*." Refer to *Siyaar A'laamin-Nubalaa* (9/442) and *at-Tahdheeb* (11/161).

3. Hammaad ibn Zayd ibn Dirham al-Azdee, Abu Ismaa'eel. He was a reliable scholar and the narrator of *hadeeth* of his time from Basrah. He died in 179 H. Ibn Mahdee said, "I did not see anyone who did not used to record in writing having better memory than him. I did not see anyone more knowledgeable than him in al-Basrah, nor did I see anyone more knowledgeable of the *Sunnah*." Refer to *Siyaar A'laamin-Nubalaa* (7/456).

4. Hammaad ibn Salamah ibn Deenaar, Abu Salamah. A reliable scholar and leading narrator of *hadeeth* from Basrah. He died in 167 H. Ibn Ma'een said, "If you see anyone who speaks ill of him, doubt that person's Islaam."

5. Maalik ibn Anas, Abu 'Abdullaah. He was the famous *Imaam* of al-Madeenah. He was born in 93H and died in 179H. Ash-Shaafi'ee said, "When the scholars are mentioned, Maalik is the star." Refer to *Tadhkiratul-Huffaadh* (1/207) and *Siyar A'laamin-Nubalaa* (8/48).

6. 'Abdur-Rahmaan ibn 'Amr ibn Abee 'Amr al-Awzaa'ee, Abu 'Amr. He was the famous scholar and narrator. He lived in Beirut and died in 157H at the age of 69. Abu Ishaaq al-Fazaree said, "If I were to choose a person to be in charge of this *Ummah*, I would choose al-Awzaa'ee." Refer to *Siyaar A'laamin-Nubalaa* (7/107).

7. Zaaidah ibn Qudaamah, Abus-Salt ath-Thaqafee. He was a reliable narrator and *Imaam* of the *Sunnah*. He was from Koofah and died in 160H. Al-'Ijlee said, "Reliable, a person of the *Sunnah*. He would not narrate to anyone until he asked about him. If he was a person of the *Sunnah*, he would narrate to him and if not he would not narrate to him." Refer to *Siyaar A'laamin-Nubalaa* (7/375).

If you see a man having love for Ahmad ibn Hanbal,[1] al-Hajjaaj ibn al-Minhaal[2] and Ahmad ibn Nasr[3] and mentioning good regarding them and speaking according to their sayings, then know that he is a person of the *Sunnah*.[4]

---

1. Ahmad ibn Muhammad ibn Hanbal, Abu 'Abdullaah. The famous scholar, Defender of the *Sunnah* and Imaam of *Ahl us-Sunnah*. He was lashed mercilessly for refusing to renounce the correct belief that the Qur'aan is the uncreated Word of Allaah. Amongst his works, one of the most well-known is the *Musnad* which contains around 40,000 *ahaadeeth*. He died in 241H at the age of 77. Refer to *Siyaar A'laamin-Nubalaa* (11/177).

2. Al-Hajjaaj ibn Minhaal al-Anmaatee, Abu Muhammad. A reliable narrator of Basrah and companion of the *Sunnah*. He died in 217 H. Khalf Kurdoos said, "Hajjaaj was a person of the *Sunnah*, he manifested it." Refer to *at-Tahdheeb* (2/206) and *Siyaar A'laamin-Nubalaa* (10/352).

3. Ahmad ibn Nasr ibn Maalik al-Khuzaa'ee. A reliable scholar and narrator. He was martyred in the time of al-Waathiq, in the year 231H, for refusing to say that the Qur'aan was created. Ibn Ma'een said, "Allaah granted that his life was ended with martyrdom," Refer to *Siyar A'laamin-Nubalaa* (11/66) and *at-Tahdheeb* (1/87).

4. The author gives these names as examples, not merely so that we should love them for their own sake, to the exclusion of others, but rather, he mentions them as examples of the scholars of the *Sunnah*, whom we should love for their adherence to the *Sunnah*.

91

144 If you see a man sitting with one of the people of innovation, warn and inform him. If he sits with him after knowing, beware of him, for he is a person of desires.[1]

---

1. Abu Daawood as-Sijjistaanee said: I said to Abu 'Abdullaah, Ahmad ibn Hanbal, 'If I see a man from *Ahl us-Sunnah* sitting with a man from the people of innovation, should I abandon speaking to him?' He said, "No, you should first inform him that the one whom you saw him with is a person of innovation. Either, he will cease speaking to him, so then continue speaking to him or if not, then regard him to be like him. Ibn Mas'ood said: A person is like his friend." Reported by Ibn Abee Ya'laa in *Tabaqaatul-Hanaabilah* (1/60) with a *saheeh isnaad* and by Ibn Muflih in *al-Aadaabush-Shar'iyyah* (1/263).

Ibn 'Awn, *rahimahullaah*, said, "Whoever sits with the people of innovation is worse than them." Reported by Ibn Battah in *al-Ibaanatul-Kubraa* (no.486).

'Alee ibn Abee Khaalid said: I said to Ahmad, "This old man - referring to an old man who was present with us and was a neighbour of mine - I have warned him against a person, but he would like to hear your saying about him. Haarith al-Qaseer (meaning Haarith al-Mahaasibee) and you saw me with him many years ago and you said to me, 'Do not sit with him and do not speak to him.' I have not spoken to him from then until now, but this old man sits with him. What do you say about him (i.e. the innovator)?" I saw that Ahmad became red, his veins and his eyes swelled. I have never seen him like that before. Then he shuddered and said, "That is one to whom Allaah has done such and such. No one knows that except one who is fully acquainted with him. Alas! Alas! Alas! He is one not known except to one fully acquainted with him. He was the one whom al-Maghaazilee sat with and Ya'qoob and so and so. He lead them to having the views of Jahm. They were destroyed through him." So, the old man said, "O Abu 'Abdullaah! He narrates *hadeeth*, displays dignity and fearfulness. He is such and such." Abu 'Abdullaah became angry and said, "Do not be fooled by his fearfulness, nor his gentleness. Do not be fooled by how he droops his head. He is an evil person. This will not be known except by one well-acquainted with him. Do not sit with him, for there is no honour for him. Will you sit with everyone who narrates the *ahaadeeth* of Allaah's Messenger (ﷺ) and is an innovator?!" Reported by Ibn Abee Ya'laa in *Tabaqaatul-Hanaabilah* (1/233-234) in the biography of 'Alee ibn Abee Khaalid.

92

145   If you hear a man to whom a narration is brought and he doesn't want to accept it, preferring the Qur'aan instead, do not doubt that he is a man who has embraced heresy, so stand up and leave him.[1]

146   Know that all innovations are despicable and invite towards using the sword.[2] The most despicable and steeped in disbelief are the *Raafidees,* the *Mu'tazilah* and the *Jahmiyyah,* since they lead the people into denial (of Allaah's attributes) and apostasy.

---

1. One who claims to believe in the Qur'aan but not in the *Sunnah* has disbelieved in the Qur'aan also, since the Qur'aan orders obedience to everything which the Prophet (ﷺ) commanded.

Abu Qilaabah said, "If you speak to a man about the *Sunnah,* but he says, 'Leave this and give us the Book of Allaah,' know that he is astray." Reported by adh-Dhahabee in *Siyaar A'laamin-Nubalaa* (4/472). Adh-Dhahabee comments, "I say: If you see a person of rhetoric, an innovator saying, 'Leave the Book and the *aahaad ahaadeeth* and give us from the intellect ('*aql*),' know that he is Abu Jahl."

2. Abu Qilaabah, *rahimahullaah,* said, "A people never introduce an innovation, except that they make use of the sword lawful."

He, *rahimahullaah,* also said, "The people of the innovated sects are people of misguidance. I do not see them except heading for the Fire. If you test them, you will see that not one of them holds a view except that it leads to their young men using the sword. Hypocrisy is of different types (he then recited *Aayaat* 75, 58 and 61 of *Soorah* at-Tawbah):

$$وَمِنْهُم مَّنْ عَٰهَدَ ٱللَّهَ$$

Of them are some who made a covenant with Allaah.

$$وَمِنْهُم مَّن يَلْمِزُكَ فِى ٱلصَّدَقَٰتِ$$

Of them are some who accuse you in the matter of (the distribution of) charity.

$$وَمِنْهُمُ ٱلَّذِينَ يُؤْذُونَ ٱلنَّبِىَّ$$

Among them are men who hurt the Messenger.

=

93

147 Know that anyone who tries to attack any of the Companions of Muhammad (ﷺ) really seek to attack Muhammad (ﷺ) and have caused harm to him in his grave.[1]

148 If anything of innovation appears in a person, beware of him, since what is hidden from you is more than what is apparent.[2]

149 However, if you see a person whose manner and opinion is despicable, he is wicked, sinful and oppressive, yet he is a person of the *Sunnah*, accompany him and sit with him, since his sin will not harm you.[3]

So their sayings, i.e. the hypocrites, varied but they were together upon doubt and declaring truth to be falsehood. These ones (the people of innovation) have different sayings, but they are together upon the (use of) the sword. I do not see them except heading for the Fire." Reported by ad-Daarimee (1/44) with a *saheeh isnaad.*

Abu Qilaabah: 'Abdullaah ibn Zayd ibn 'Amr, Abu 'Aamir al-Jarmee. He was one of the scholars of the *taabi'een* who lived in Basrah. He fled from his land when he was sought to be appointed as the chief judge. He died in 104H or 107H. Refer to *Siyaar A'laamin-Nubalaa* (4/468).

1. Al-Fudayl ibn 'Iyaad said, "Indeed, I love those whom Allaah loves. They are those from whom the Companions of Muhammad (ﷺ) are safe. I hate those whom Allaah hates. They are the people of the deviant sects and innovation." (Abu Nu'aym in *al-Hilyah* (8/103) with a *saheeh isnaad).*

2. Al-Barbahaaree, *rahimahullaah,* said, "The innovators are like scorpions. They bury their heads and bodies in the sand and leave their tails out. When they get the chance they sting; the same with the innovators who conceal themselves amongst the people, when they are able, they do what they desire." Reported in *Tabaaqatul-Hanaabilah* (2/44) and *Manhajul-Ahmad.*

3. The author is explaining the seriousness and danger of innovated beliefs and sitting with and listening to the people who hold these beliefs and that this is more dangerous than sitting with even the people of sin. This does not mean that there is no harm in sitting with sinners, rather, it is to be feared that one who sits with sinners will have the sins they commit made alluring to him by Shaitaan, until he regards the sins as lawful and is destroyed, since one who declares forbidden acts to be lawful has left Islaam. Rather, he should only sit with them if his intention is to call them to repent and give them *da'wah,* provided he thinks that he will not be affected by them.

If you see a man who strives hard and long in worship, is abstemious, being continual in worship, except that he is a person of innovation, do not sit with him, do not listen to his words and do not walk along with him, since I do not feel safe, that you will not eventually come to be pleased with his way and go to destruction along with him.[1]

Yunus ibn 'Ubaid saw a son of his come out from the house of an innovator, so he said to him, "O my son! Where have you come from?" He replied, "From so and so."[2] He said, "O my son! That I see you come out of the house of a shameless person is more beloved to me than that I should see you come out of the house of so and so. That you meet Allaah as a fornicator, thief and treacherous person is more beloved to me than that you meet Him with the saying of the innovators." Do you not see that Yunus knew that this shameless person would not lead his son away from the Religion, whereas, the innovator will indeed misguide him until he causes him to disbelieve!

150   Beware! Beware of the people of your time! Look to whom you sit with, hear from and accompany, for it is as if the creation have apostasised except those of them whom Allaah has protected!

---

1. Imaam ash-Shaafi'ee, *rahimahullaah*, said, "That a servant meets Allaah with every sin except *Shirk* is better than meeting Him upon any of the innovated beliefs." Reported by al-Baihaqee in *al-I'tiqaad* (p.158).

2. In the other manuscript: From 'Amr ibn 'Ubayd.

151   If you see a man speaking well of Ibn Abee Du'aad,[1] al-Mareesee,[2] Thumaamah,[3] Abul-Hudhail[4] or Hisham al-Footee or any of their followers and adherents, beware of him because he is an innovator. These people were upon apostasy, so leave this man who spoke well of them and whomever he mentioned of them.

152   To set up trials in Islaam is an innovation. As for today, people should be tested about the *Sunnah*, because of his saying, *"This is the knowledge of the Religion, so look from whom you take your Religion"*[5] and, *"Do not accept hadeeth except from those whose witness you would accept."*[6] So look and see if he is a person of the *Sunnah* with comprehension and is truthful then write from him and if not then leave him.

---

1. Ibn Abee Du'aad, the Jahmee, the caller to the belief that the Qur'aan is created. He perished in 240H.
2. Bishr ibn Ghiyaath al-Mareesee. He was the head of the *Jahmiyyah* in his time. He was declared to be a disbeliever by a number of the scholars. He perished in 218H.
3. Thumaamah ibn Ashras al-Basree. He was one of the heads of the Mu'tazilah and believed that the Qur'aan was created.
4. Muhammad ibn Hudayl al-'Allaaf al-Basree. He was a head of innovation and a caller to it in his time. He perished in 227H.
5. This is the saying of the *tabi'ee*, Muhammad ibn Seereen. It is reported by Muslim in the introduction to his *Saheeh* and by Abu Nu'aym in *al-Hilyah* (2/278). It is also reported as a *marfoo' hadeeth* by Ibn 'Adiyy in *al-Kaamil* (1/155) and others, but it is very weak.
6. Reported as a *marfoo' hadeeth* by ar-Raamaahurmuzee in *al-Muhaddithul-Faadil* (p.411), Ibn 'Adiyy in *al-Kaamil* and al-Khateeb in *al-Kifaayah* (pp.125-126). It is declared to be a fabrication (*mawdoo'*) by al-Albaanee in *Da'eef ul-Jaami'* (no.6193).

153   If you wish to be firm upon the truth and the way of *Ahl us-Sunnah* before you, beware of theological rhetoric (*Kalaam*) and the people of theological rhetoric and of disputation, arguing, analogy and debating about the Religion. Listening to them, even if you do not accept from them, throws doubt into the heart. This is sufficient for you to be destroyed. There has never been any heresy, innovation, innovated sect or misguidance except through rhetoric, disputation,[1] argumentation and analogy. These are the gates of innovation, doubt and heresy.

154   By Allaah, beware of Allaah concerning yourself and stick to the narrations, the people of narrations and to following, for the Religion is to follow, meaning the Prophet (ﷺ) and his Companions, may Allaah be pleased with them all. Those before us have not left us in a confused state, so follow them and be at peace. Do not exceed the narrations and the people of narrations.

155   Withhold about those things (from the Qur'aan and the *ahaadeeth*) whose meaning is unclear. Do not use analogy on anything.[2]

---

1. The Messenger of Allaah (ﷺ) said, *"A people have never gone astray except that they were given to disputation."* He (ﷺ) then recited:

$$مَاضَرَبُوهُ لَكَ إِلَّا جَدَلًا ۚ بَلْ هُمْ قَوْمٌ خَصِمُونَ ۝$$

They mention this to you, only by way of disputation. No! But they are a quarrelsome people."
                                                            Soorah az-Zukhruf (43):58

Reported by Ahmad (5/252 and 256), at-Tirmidhee (no. 3250) and Ibn Maajah (no. 48). Declared *saheeh* by Shaikh al-Albaanee in his checking of *al-Mishkaat* (no. 18) and *Saheehul-Jaami'* (no. 5509).
   This point contains a prohibition of disputation but does not forbid what is necessary as regards rebutting and replying to the doubts and false beliefs spread by the innovators.
   2. Opinion and analogy have no place in matters of *'Aqeedah*.

156   Do not seek to invent a means of replying to the innovators, since you are ordered to face them with silence and not to open yourself up to them. Do you not know that Muhammad ibn Seereen, along with his excellence, did not reply to a certain innovator about a single question and would not even listen to him recite a verse from the Book of Allaah, the Mighty and Majestic. He was asked (as to why he would not listen to the innovator recite from the Book of Allaah). He said, "I fear that he would twist it and that something of that would fall into my heart."[1]

157   If you hear a man say, 'Indeed we declare Allaah greater,'[2] when he hears the narrations[3] from the Messenger of Allaah (ﷺ), know that he is a *Jahmee*. He wishes to reject the sayings of Allaah's Messenger (ﷺ) and refuse them through this saying of theirs, claiming that they are exalting Allaah and declaring Him free from imperfections when they hear the *hadeeth* about seeing Allaah (in the Hereafter) and about His descending etc. Has he not rejected the narrations from the Messenger of Allaah (ﷺ)? By saying, 'We exalt Allaah above descending from place to place,' he claims that he knows about Allaah better than others.[4]

---

1. Reported by ad-Daarimee (1/91), Ibn Waddah in *al-Bida'h* (p.53), al-Aajurree in *ash-Sharee'ah* (p.57), al-Laalikaa'ee in *as-Sunnah* (no.242) and *al-Ibaanatul-Kubraa* (pp.398-399) and is *saheeh*.

2. What they mean is that they think that these attributes do not befit Allaah, the Most High, so they deny them!

3. Those narrations affirming the attributes of Allaah.

4. If only they clung to the way of the *Salaf* and said, "We affirm all of Allaah's attributes which He affirmed for Himself or which His Messenger (ﷺ) affirmed for Him, in a manner befitting His Majesty, not like the attributes of creation." Just as we affirm Allaah's existence, but say it is not like the existence of the creation.

Beware of these people, because most of the common people and others are upon this state. Warn the people against them (i.e. the *Jahmiyyah*). If anyone asks you about a question in this book, seeking to know, speak to him and teach him. However, if someone comes to debate with you, beware of him. For debating involves argumentation, disputing, seeking to overcome, wrangling and anger. You have been forbidden from all of this. It diverts you both away from the truth. It has not reached us that any of our scholars or people of knowledge argued, debated or disputed.

Al-Hasan (al-Basree) said, "The wise man does not argue or seek to overcome with stratagem rather he propagates his wisdom. If it is accepted he praises Allaah and if it is rejected he praises Allaah."[1]

A man came to al-Hasan (al-Basree) and said, "I wish to debate with you about the Religion." Al-Hasan replied, "I know my Religion. If you have lost your Religion go out and look for it!"[2]

The Messenger of Allaah (ﷺ) heard some people arguing outside his apartment, one of them saying, 'Did not Allaah say so and so ?' and the other saying, 'Did not Allaah say so and so ?' So he came out angry and said, *"Is this what I have ordered you, or is this what I was sent with, that you should set one part of the Book of Allaah against some other parts ?"*[3] So he forbade them from argumentation.

---

1. Reported by Nu'aym ibn Hammaad in his *Zawaa'id 'alaz-Zuhd libnil-Mubaarak* (no.30) and Ibn Battah in *Ibaanatul-Kubraa* (no.611). Its *isnaad* is weak, since it contains an unnamed narrator.
2. Reported by al-Aajurree in *ash-Sharee'ah* (p.57), al-Laalikaa'ee in *as-Sunnah* (no.215) and Ibn Battah (no.586) and it is *saheeh*.
3. Reported by Ahmad (2/178, 181 and 196), Ibn Maajah (no. 85), 'Abdullaah ibn Ahmad in *as-Sunnah* (no. 86) and al-Baghawee in *Sharhus-Sunnah* (1/260). Al-Boosayree declared it *saheeh* in *Zawaa'id Ibn Maajah* (1/4) as did al-Albaanee in *Sharh 'Aqeedah at-Tahaawiyyah* (p.218).

Ibn 'Umar used to hate disputation as did Maalik ibn Anas and those greater and lesser than him right up to this day.

The Saying of Allaah, the Mighty and Majestic, is greater than the sayings of His creation. Allaah, the Most High says:

مَا يُجَٰدِلُ فِىٓ ءَايَٰتِ ٱللَّهِ إِلَّا ٱلَّذِينَ كَفَرُوا۟

None dispute in the *Aayaat* (signs, proofs) of Allaah except those who disbelieve.[1]

A man asked 'Umar ibn al-Khattaab: What is

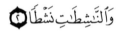

Those (angels) who gently take out (the souls of the believers)?[2]

He said, "If your head were shaved, I would have beheaded you."[3]

The Prophet (ﷺ) said, *"The Believer does not dispute and I will not intercede on the Day of Resurrection for those who dispute, so leave arguing for its lack of good."*[4]

---

1. Soorah Ghaafir (40):4
2. Soorah an-Naazi'aat (79):2.
3. Shaving the head was the sign of the *Khawaarij*. The man who asked 'Umar was called Sabeegh. His story is well-known and authentic. It is reported by ad-Daarimee (1/51), Ibn Waddah in *al-Bida'h* (p.56), al-Aajurree in *ash-Sharee'ah* (p.73), al-Laalikaa'ee in *as-Sunnah* (pp. 634-636) and Ibn Battah (1/414-415).
4. This *hadeeth* is very weak, as declared by al-Haithumee in *Majma' uz-Zawaa'id* (1/156, 7/259). Reported by at-Tabaraanee in *al-Kabeer* (8/178-179) and al-Aajurree in *ash-Sharee'ah* (pp. 55-56).

158 It is not permitted for a man to say, 'So and so is a person of the *Sunnah*' until he knows that he combines the characteristics of the *Sunnah*, so it is not said of him, 'a person of the *Sunnah*' until he combines all of the *Sunnah*.

159 'Abdullaah ibn al-Mubaarak said, "The roots of the seventy two innovated sects are four sects; and from these four the seventy two sects spread. (The four being) the *Qadariyyah*, the *Murjiah*, the *Shee'ah* and the *Khawaarij*."[1]

Whoever gives precedence to Abu Bakr, 'Umar, 'Uthmaan and 'Alee over the rest of the Companions of Allaah's Messenger (ﷺ) and does not speak about the rest except with good and supplicates for them has escaped *Shi'ism*; its beginning and its end.

He who says that *Eemaan* is saying and action and it increases and decreases has escaped *Irjaa*; its beginning and its end.

He who says that Prayer is to be performed behind every (*Imaam*), pious or wicked, that *Jihaad* is to be fought along with every *Khaleefah* and he does not hold it permissible to oppose the ruler with the sword and he makes supplication for them to be upright has escaped the saying of the *Khawaarij*; its beginning and its end.

He who says that everything occurs by the Pre-decree (*Qadr*) of Allaah, the Mighty and Majestic, the good and the bad, He guides whom He pleases and misguides whom He pleases, has escaped the saying of the *Qadariyyah*; its beginning and its end. He is a person of the *Sunnah*.

---

1. Reported by Ibn Battah in *Ibaanatul-Kubraa* (no.278).

160   The return to this world of those who have died (*ar-raj'ah*) is an innovation and is disbelief in Allaah, the Sublime. Whoever professes to believe it, is a disbeliever in Allaah and in this there is no doubt.[1] Whoever believes in *ar-raj'ah* and says that 'Alee ibn Abee Taalib is alive and will return before the Day of Resurrection and says the same concerning Muhammad ibn 'Alee, Ja'far ibn Muhammad and Moosaa ibn Ja'far and talks about the station of the *Imaams* and that they know the unseen, beware of them! They are disbelievers in Allaah, the Sublime.[2]

161   Ta'mah ibn 'Amr[3] and Sufyaan ibn 'Uyainah[4] said, "Whoever withholds judgement with regard to 'Uthmaan and 'Alee,[5] he is a *Shee'ee*. He is not to be held as reliable, nor spoken to, nor sat with. Whoever prefers 'Alee over 'Uthmaan is a *Raafidee*, who rejects the narrations from the Companions of Allaah's Messenger (ﷺ).

---

1. Refer to *Mysteries of the Soul Expounded* by Abu Bilal Mustafa al-Kanadi (pp.51-76).
2. Refer to what Abul-Hasan al-Ash'aree, *rahimahullaah,* wrote in *al-Maqaalaat* about this depraved sect. In the English language, the following works document and refute the beliefs of this sect: *The Devils Deception of the Shee'ah* by Ibn al-Jawzee, translated by Abu Ameenah Bilal Philips, *al-Khutootul-'Areedah*, *The Mirage in Iran* by Dr. A. Afghaanee, translated by Abu Ameenah Bilal Philips and the works of Ihsan Ilahi Zaheer, *rahimahullaah,* such as *The Shi'ites and the Sunnah* and *The House of Ali.*
3. Ta'mah ibn 'Amr al-Ja'faree. A worshipper and a reliable scholar and narrator of *hadeeth* from Koofah. He died in 169 H. Refer to *at-Tahdheeb* (5/13).
4. Sufyaan ibn 'Uyainah ibn Maimoon al-Hilaalee, Abu Muhammad. Originally from Koofah but moved to Makkah. He was one of the great and famous scholars and was an Imaam of *Hadeeth, Sunnah* and *fiqh*. He died in 198H at the age of 91. Imaam Ahmad said, "I have not seen anyone more knowledgeable of the practices of the *Sunnah* than him." Refer to *Siyar 'Alaamin-Nubalaa* (8/454).
5. i.e. does not give 'Uthmaan his due precedence over 'Alee. May Allaah be pleased with them both.

Whoever gives precedence to the three[1] over the rest of them and supplicates for Allaah's mercy upon the rest and withholds regarding their slips, he is upon the correct path and guidance in this matter."

162 The *Sunnah* is to bear witness of Paradise for the ten for whom Allaah's Messenger (ﷺ) bore witness that they will be in Paradise.[2] There is no doubt about it.

163 Do not particularise anyone with supplication for Allaah's praises (*salaat*) except the Messenger of Allaah.[3]

164 Know that 'Uthmaan was murdered unjustly. The one who killed him was an unjust oppressor.

165 Whoever affirms and believes what is contained in this book and takes it as an example to be followed, does not doubt about any of it or deny any of it, is a person of the *Sunnah* and the *Jamaa'ah* and the *Sunnah* is complete in him. Whoever denies, doubts about any of this book or withholds judgement, is a person of innovation.[4]

---

1. The three whom are referred to here are Abu Bakr, 'Umar and 'Uthmaan, *radiallaahu 'anhum*.

2. 'Abdur-Rahmaan ibn 'Awf reports that Allaah's Messenger (ﷺ) said, *"Abu Bakr is in Paradise; 'Umar is in Paradise; 'Uthmaan is in Paradise; 'Alee is in Paradise; Talhah is in Paradise; az-Zubayr is in Paradise; 'Abdur-Rahmaan ibn 'Awf is in Paradise; Sa'd ibn Abee Waqqaas is in Paradise; Sa'eed ibn Zayd is in Paradise and Abu 'Ubaydah ibn al-Jarraah is in Paradise."* Reported by Ahmad and at-Tirmidhee (no.4012) and is *saheeh*.

3. The supplication referred to here is *sallallaahu 'alaihi (wa sallam)* (ﷺ). In addition, we also supplicate for Allaah's *salaat* upon the previous Prophets and Messengers, *salawaatullaahi wa salaamuhu 'alaihim*. Refer to *Jalaa' ul-Afhaam* (p.345) of Ibn al-Qayyim and *Tafseer Ibn Katheer* (3/516-517) and *al-Qawlul-Badee'* (pp.81-87) of as-Sakhaawee.

4. What is meant here is that if one rejects anything from the Book of Allaah, the authentic *Sunnah* and the understanding of the *Salaf*.

166   Whoever denies or doubts a single letter of the Qur'aan or anything from Allaah's Messenger (ﷺ) will meet Allaah as a denier (of the truth). Fear Allaah, take warning and take care of your Faith!

167   From the *Sunnah* is that you do not help anyone in disobedience to Allaah, whether they be parents or any of the creation. There is no obedience to a human in disobedience to Allaah and no one is to be loved for that (i.e. disobedience to Allaah). Rather all of that is to be hated for (the sake of) Allaah, the Blessed and Most High.[1]

168   To believe that repentance is obligatory upon the worshippers. They should repent to Allaah, the Mighty and Majestic, from major and minor sins.[2]

169   Whoever will not bear witness of Paradise for those whom the Messenger of Allaah bore witness for, is a person of innovation and misguidance, doubting about what the Messenger of Allaah said.

---

1. 'Alee, *radiallaahu 'anhu*, reports that the Messenger of Allaah (ﷺ) said, *"There is no obedience to the creation, in disobedience to the Creator. Obedience is only in what is good."* Reported by al-Bukhaaree and Muslim (Eng. trans. 3/1022/no.4536).

2. The conditions for repentance are:
(i) Giving up the sin.
(ii) Remorse.
(iii) Resolving not to repeat the sin.
(iv) Compensating for any wrong that may have been done to anyone.
Refer to *Salvation Through Repentance* by Abu Ameenah Bilal Philips and *I would like to repent, But!* by Muhammad Saleh al-Munajjid, translated by Syed Iqbal Zaheer.

170 Maalik ibn Anas said, "He who keeps to the *Sunnah* and he from who the Companions of Allaah's Messenger are safe, will be with the Prophets, the truthful witnesses, the martyrs and the righteous ones when he dies, even if he falls short in action."

Bishr ibn Haarith[1] said, "Islaam is the *Sunnah* and the *Sunnah* is Islaam."

Al-Fudayl ibn 'Iyaad said, "If I see a man from the people of *Sunnah*, it is as if I have seen a man from the Companions of the Messenger of Allaah (ﷺ). If I see a man of innovation, it is as if I have seen a man from the hypocrites."

Yunus ibn 'Ubaid said, "How remarkable today are those who call to the *Sunnah*. Even more remarkable are those who respond and accept the *Sunnah*."[2]

Ibn 'Awn repeatedly said at the point of death, "The *Sunnah*, The *Sunnah* and beware of innovation" until he died.

Ahmad ibn Hanbal said, "A man of my companions died and was seen in a dream saying: say to Abu 'Abdullaah,[3] "Stick to the *Sunnah*, for the first thing that my Lord, the Mighty and Majestic, asked me about was the *Sunnah*."[4]

---

1. Bishr ibn al-Haarith al-Marwazee, Abu Nasr. A reliable scholar and narrator from Baghdaad. He died in 227H at the age of 76. Refer to *Siyar A'laamin-Nubalaa* (10/469).

2. Reported by Abu Nu'aym in *al-Hilyah* (3/21) and Ibn Battah in *al-Ibaanatul-Kubraa* (no.20) and al-Laalikaa'ee in *as-Sunnah* (nos.21,22,23).

3. i.e. Imaam Ahmad.

4. Dreams can only be used to reinforce what we already know with certainty from the Religion, such as the obligation of sticking to the *Sunnah*. As regards to changing *Sharee'ah* rulings or making additions or deletions to the Religion none of this can be done, since the Religion has already been perfected and completed.

Abul 'Aaliyah said, "Whoever dies unknown upon the *Sunnah* is indeed a truthful witness. It is said clinging to the *Sunnah* is salvation."

Sufyaan ath-Thawree said, "Whoever listens to a person of innovation has left the protection of Allaah and is entrusted to it - meaning the innovation."[1]

Daawood ibn Abee Hind[2] said, "Allaah, the Blessed and Most High, revealed to Moosaa ibn 'Imraan: Do not sit with the people of innovation, for if you were to sit with them and something of what they say took root in your heart, I would throw you into the Fire of Hell."[3]

Al-Fudayl ibn 'Iyaad said, "Whoever sits with a person of innovation has not been given wisdom."[4]

Al-Fudayl ibn 'Iyaad said, "Do not sit with an innovator for I fear that curses will descend upon you."[5]

---

1. Reported by Abu Nu'aym in *al-Hilyah* (7/26,34) and Ibn Battah in *al-Ibaanatul-Kubraa* (no.444).
2. Daawood ibn Abee Hind al-Quraishee, Abu Bakr or Abu Muhammad. A scholar and precise narrator from Basrah. He died in 140 H. See *Siyar A'laamin-Nubalaa* (6/376).
3. Reported by Ibn Waddaah (no.49) with its like from Muhammad ibn Aslam.
4. Reported by al-Laalikaa'ee (no. 263) and Ibn Battah (no.439) and its *isnaad* is *saheeh*.
5. Reported by al-Laalikaa'ee (no. 262) and Ibn Battah (nos.441,451) and its *isnaad* is *saheeh*.

Al-Fudayl ibn 'Iyaad said, "Whoever loves a person of innovation then Allaah renders his actions futile and takes away the light of Islaam from his heart."[1]

Al-Fudayl ibn 'Iyaad said, "Whoever sits in a road with a person of innovation, take a different road."[2]

Al-Fudayl ibn 'Iyaad said, "Whoever honours an innovator has assisted in the demolition of Islaam."[3]

Al-Fudayl ibn 'Iyaad said, "Whoever smiles in the face of an innovator has made light of what Allaah, the Mighty and Majestic, sent down upon Muhammad (ﷺ). Whoever marries his beloved daughter to an innovator has cut off her ties of relationship.[4] Whoever follows the funeral procession of an innovator does not cease to be under the wrath of Allaah until he returns."

Al-Fudayl ibn 'Iyaad said, "I would eat with a Jew or a Christian but not with an innovator. I would like that there was between myself and a person of innovation, a protected fort of iron."[5]

---

1. Reported by al-Laalikaa'ee (no. 263) and Ibn Battah (no.440), Abu Nu'aym in al-Hilyah (8/103) and Ibn al-Jawzee in Talbees Iblees (p.16) with a saheeh isnaad.

2. Reported by Ibn Battah (no.493), Abu Nu'aym in al-Hilyah (8/103) and Ibn al-Jawzee in Talbees Iblees (p.16) with a saheeh isnaad.

3. This has also been reported as the saying of the Prophet (ﷺ). However, it is not authentic, as explained by Shaikh al-Albaanee in as-Silsilatud-Da'eefah (no.1862). It is also reported as the saying of the taabi'ee, Ibraaheem ibn Maysarah (d.132H) by al-Laalikaa'ee.

4. Reported by Abu Nu'aym in al-Hilyah (8/103) and Ibn al-Jawzee in Talbees Iblees (p.16) (except the last sentence) with a saheeh isnaad.

5. Reported by al-Laalikaa'ee (no. 1149), Abu Nu'aym in al-Hilyah (8/103) and Ibn Battah (no.470) reports the second part and its isnaad is saheeh.

Al-Fudayl ibn 'Iyaad said, "If Allaah, (the Mighty and Majestic), knows that a man hates a person of innovation, He will forgive him even if his actions are few.[1] A person of *Sunnah* would not help an innovator except due to hypocrisy.[2] Whoever turns his face away from an innovator, Allaah will fill his heart with Faith. Whoever frightens an innovator away, Allaah will grant him safety on the Day of Great Terror and whoever debases an innovator, Allaah will raise him in Paradise by a hundred ranks, So, for Allaah, never shelter an innovator !"

THE END

---

1. This part is reported by Abu Nu'aym in *al-Hilyah* (8/103) with a *saheeh isnaad* and his version ends, "...then I hope that he will be forgiven."
2. Its like is reported by Abu Nu'aym in *al-Hilyah* (8/104) with a *saheeh isnaad*. It is reported as worded here by Ibn Battah (no.429) with an acceptable *isnaad*.

Appendix 1

Examples of the Pages of the Manuscript

The Title Page

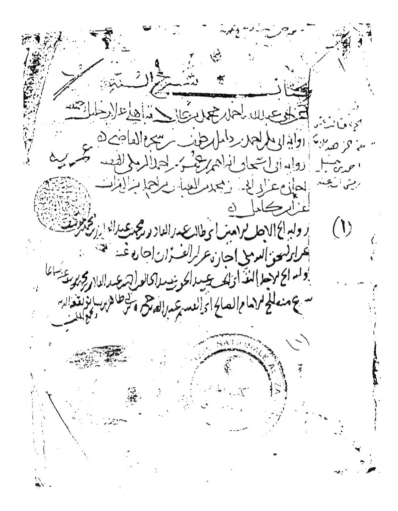

بسم الله الرحمن الرحيم

قال الشيخ الإمام السعيد أبو الحسين علي بن عبد الغني بن عبد الخالق فلان الخراط طيب

عبد الله بن محمد بن عبد القادر بن محمد بن يوسف بالمسجد الجامع وهو

يسمع كل له أحمد بكم الحج إلى إسحاق بن شهير بن عمر بن أحمد الثعلبي فيما

أذن لكم من روايته عنه وأجازه لكم واعزف ذلك وقال فتح ما

أبنا أبو الحسن محمد بن العباس براجد القراآت حدالله في كتابه وفي

كتابه نزي قال أنا أبو الطاهر أبو الحسن كامل بن طيف بركم القاضي قرأ عليه

قال ندفع إلى أبو عبد الله أحمد بن محمد بن عايد أبنا هذا الدابر وقال

بإسناده حتى هذا الدابر من أوله إلى آخره ثم قال أبو عبد الله أحمد بن

محمد بن عايد الماهر أرضى السعيد الحميد الذي هدانا للإسلام

وشرع علمنا به وأخبرنا وجنبنا عنه ثم سلمه النبوي للمجيد ورضا

والحفظ ما لله وسخطه ما علوا أن الإسلام هو السنة وأنه

هو الإسلام ولا تقوم أحدهما بالآخر فمن السنة لزوم الجماعة

فمن دعا بغير الجماعة وفارضها فقد خلع ربقة الإسلام من عنقه

وصار صالا مضلا د والأسا سر الذي بناه على الجماعة وقفه

وطاعة الله ساك فيما قال رسول الله صلى الله عليه وسلم وقال عطاء من انقرض من السنة
وبقي من اصحاب رسول الله صلى الله عليه وسلم فهؤلاء كانوا مع البشير والنذير
والشهداء والصالحين وان كان في عصره في العمل وقال رسول الله الحزن
الاسلام هو والسنة والسنة هي الاسلام وقال فضيل بن عياض
اذا رأيت طلام اهل السنة فكأنما ارى طلام اصحاب رسول الله صلى الله
واذا رأيت طلام اهل البدع فكأنما ارى طلام المنافقين وقال
يونس بن عبد الحبيب من ابتدعوا اليوم الى السنة واجعلها منه
تحببوا الى السنة فيقبل له وكان ابرعون يقول عند الموت السنة
السنة واياكم والبدع حتى مات وقال ابو عبد الله علام خليل
ومات رطلام من اصحابي في يرسنه المنام وقال قولوا الابي عبد الله
عليك بالسنة فان اول ما يسالنج الله السائلج عن السنة وقال ابو
العالية من خصال على السنة منشور او مصدق وقال الاعتصام
بالسنة نجاه ة   اخر الكتاب   والحمد لله رب العالمين وصلواته على محمد وآله

وصوم السماع والاحاديث . تسع عبد العزيز حمد ركسانو
اسمع جمعة الحجار طالب ابن الله مراد محمد بن اصر محمد على اولاد احمد ابو الرشد
والبرا المحالة ابو الفرح ير بسف موا احدار الفرح الدروان الادب ابو منصور الجوالبع والابو الدلهم
رار الالفا الملط المهوى ابو الفرح عبد الخالوي احمد بعد الماذ روا عبد الغنى على ابن الصحى
الحاظ والبرا العصل المهوى وصاحب المطبع وهار رست الهروى احمد عبد الفيز على وحمر رارث
رجا على احمد بسع محمد ابن احمد بعد ابه اود الاصمعى الدلكى بنت سعد اهل المرد وحباب

Appendix 2

Allaah's Ascension (al-Istiwaa') over the Throne

The Aayaat of the Qur'aan

Allaah, the Most High, says:

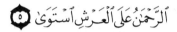

The Most Merciful ascended above the Throne.

Soorah Taa-Haa (20):5

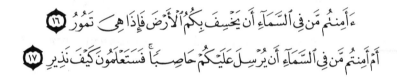

Do you feel secure that He Who is above the heavens will not cause you to be swallowed up by the earth when it shakes (as in an earthquake)? Or do you feel secure that He who is above the heavens will not send against you a violent tornado? Then you shall know how (terrible) was My warning.

Soorah al-Mulk (67):16-17

The Ahaaheeth of the Prophet (ﷺ)

The Prophet (ﷺ) asked (the slave girl), *"Where is Allaah?"* She replied, "He is above the sky." He (ﷺ) asked (her), *"Who am I?"* She said, "You are Allaah's Messenger." He (ﷺ) said (to her master), *"Free her, for she is a believer."* Reported by Muslim (1/537).

Abu Sa'eed al-Khudree reports that the Messenger of Allaah (ﷺ) said, *"Do you not trust me and I am the trustworthy servant of Him who is above the sky. The news of heaven comes to me in the morning and in the evening."* Reported by al-Bukhaaree (8/67) and Muslim (2/742).

The Sayings of the Pious Predecessors

Abu Bakr, *radiallaahu 'anhu*

'Abdullaah ibn 'Umar, *radiallaahu 'anhu,* reports that when Allaah's Messenger (ﷺ) was taken, Abu Bakr, *radiallaahu 'anhu,* entered and kissed his (ﷺ) forehead and said, "May my father and mother be your ransom! You were good in life and in death." And he said, "He who worshipped Muhammad, then Muhammad has died. (But) he who worships Allaah, then Allaah is above the sky, He lives and does not die." Reported by ad-Daarimee in *ar-Radd 'alal Jahmiyyah,* with a *hasan isnaad.*

Imaam Maalik, *Imaam* of Daaril-Hijrah (d.179H)

'Abdullaah ibn Naafi' reports that Maalik ibn Anas said, "Allaah is above the sky and His knowledge is in every place, not being absent from anything." Reported by 'Abdullaah ibn Ahmad in *as-Sunnah* (p.5), Abu Daawood in *al-Masaa'il* (p.263), al-Aajurree in *ash-Sharee'ah* (p.289) and al-Laalikaa'ee (1/92/2). Its *isnaad* is *saheeh.*

'Abdullaah ibn al-Mubaarak, Shaikh ul-Islaam (d.181H)

'Alee ibn al-Hasan ibn Shaqeeq reports: I asked 'Abdullaah ibn al-Mubaarak, "How are we to know our Lord?" He replied, "He is above the seventh heaven above his Throne. We do not say as the

Jahmiyyah say, 'He is here on the earth.'" So that was mentioned to Ahmad ibn Hanbal, so he said, 'That is how it is with us.'

Reported by ad-Daarimee in *ar-Radd 'alal-Mareesee* (p.24 and 103) and *ar-Radd 'alal-Jahmiyyah* (p.50) and 'Abdullaah ibn Ahmad in *as-Sunnah* (p.7,25,35 and 72). Its *isnaad* is *saheeh*.

Imaam Muhammad ibn Idrees ash-Shaafi'ee (d.204H)

Abu Thawr and Abu Shu'aib both report that ash-Shaafi'ee said, "The saying which I hold regarding the *Sunnah* and which I found those whom I have seen holding like Sufyaan, Maalik and others is: the testification that none has the right to be worshipped but Allaah and that Muhammad is the Messenger of Allaah, that Allaah is above His Throne over His heaven, He draws near to His creation as He wishes and descends to the lowest heaven as He wishes...." (*Mukhtasar al-'Uluww*, no.196).

Imaam Ahmad ibn Hanbal (d.241H)

It was said to Abu 'Abdullaah (Imaam Ahmad): Allaah is above the seventh heaven, over His Throne, separate from His creation. His Power and Knowledge are in every place? He said, "Yes, He is above the Throne and His Knowledge is in every place." Reported by al-Khallaal in *al-Mukhtasar* and its *isnaad* is *saheeh*.

These are just a few of the sayings of the scholars. Adh-Dhahabee has collected over two-hundred sayings of the early scholars in this regard in his book *al-'Uluww*. In the English language, The *Ever-Merciful Istiwa Over the Throne* by Shaikh 'Abdullah as-Sabt deals with this subject in a methodological manner. A good but brief explanation of this important belief can also be found in *Fundamentals of Tawheed* by Abu Ameenah Bilal Philips.

Appendix 3

The Sects

Mushabbihah (or **Mujassimah**): Those who declare that Allaah is like His creation and that the attributes of Allaah are like the attributes of the creation. This was first propagated by Maqaatil ibn Sulaymaan al-Khuraasaanee, during the era of the *taabi'een*.

Jahmiyyah: The followers of al-Jahm ibn Safwaan, the student of al-Ja'd ibn Dirham, both of whom were executed for their apostasy in the time of the lesser *taabi'een*. Among their beliefs is that they deny the attributes of Allaah and declare that the Qur'aan is created.

Naasibee: One who has hatred towards 'Alee and the family of the Prophet (ﷺ).

Raafidees: Extreme *Shee'ah*, who call themselves the *Ithnaa Ash'ariyyah* (The Twelvers) or *Ja'farees*. This sect was founded by 'Abdullaah ibn Saba, a Jew, who appeared in the time of the Khilaafah of 'Uthmaan. He claimed love for 'Alee and the *Ahl ul-Bayt* (the family of the Prophet (ﷺ)). They curse the Companions and declare them to be disbelievers, in particular Abu Bakr, 'Umar and 'Uthmaan and the wives of the Prophet (ﷺ). They also believe the Qur'aan to be incomplete.

Khawaarij: Those who rebelled against 'Alee, *radiallaahu 'anhu*, declaring him to be a disbeliever and those who rebel against and fight the Muslim rulers. They hold that Muslims who have committed major sins are disbelievers and are doomed to Hell-Fire forever.

Mu'tazilah: This sect began at the start of the second century after the Hijrah. It was founded by 'Amr ibn 'Ubayd and Waasil ibn 'Ataa. This sect believes in the negation of Allaah's attributes, calling it *Tawheed*! They believe the Qur'aan to be created, rebellion against the Muslim rulers to be correct and that the Muslims, guilty of major sins, are in a position between Belief and disbelief and that they are destined to be in Hell forever.

Jabariyyah (or **Mujbirah**): The *Jabariyyah* hold that people have no free-will and are not responsible for their own actions, rather they are forced.

Qadariyyah: They are also the followers of Jahm ibn Safwaan. This sect was founded by Ma'bad al-Juhanee in Basrah at the end of the era of the Companions. They deny Allaah's Pre-decree (*Qadr*) and believe that man creates his own actions which are outside the Will and Power of Allaah.

Murji'ah: They uphold the belief of *Irjaa'* (to hold that sins, major or minor, do not affect *Eemaan* (Faith) and that *Eemaan* neither increases nor decreases). The first to call to this belief was Gheelaan ibn Abee Gheelaan, the Qadariyy. He was executed in 105H. They claim that actions are not part of Faith, that people do not vary in Faith, that Faith does not increase and decrease and that one should declare himself a Believer without saying 'If Allaah wills.' The *Murji'ah* are divided into three groups, as Shaikh ul-Islaam Ibn Taimiyyah has mentioned:

(i) Those who claim that Faith is a condition of the heart only.
(ii) Those who claim that Faith is merely verbal affirmation (i.e. the Karraamiyyah).
(iii) Those who claim that Faith is only affirmation with the heart and tongue, but that action is necessary in addition to it.

Appendix 4

The Imaams of the *Sunnah*

The following is a translation from *Sharh Usool I'tiqaad Ahlis-Sunnah wal-Jamaa'ah* of al-Laalikaa'ee (d.418H), checked by Dr. Ahmad Sa'd Hamdaan (vol.1, pp.29-49):

Chapter: A mention of those described as being the *Imaams* of the *Sunnah*, *Da'wah* and guidance to the correct way after the Messenger of Allaah (ﷺ) - the *Imaam* of *Imaams*.

From the Companions[1]

Abu Bakr as-Siddeeq (d.13H), 'Umar ibn al-Khattaab (d.23H), 'Uthmaan (d.35H), 'Alee (d.40H), az-Zubayr (d.36H), Sa'eed ibn Abee Waqqaas (d.54H), Sa'eed ibn Zayd (d.50H), 'Abdur-Rahmaan ibn 'Awf (d.31H), 'Abdullaah ibn Mas'ood (d.32H), Mu'aadh ibn Jabal (d.171H), Ubayy ibn Ka'b (d.22H), Ibn 'Abbaas (d.68H), Ibn 'Umar (d.84H), 'Abdullaah ibn 'Amr ibn al-'Aas (d.65H), 'Abdullaah ibn az-Zubayr (d.73H), Zayd ibn Thaabit (d.45 or 48H), Abud-Dardaa (d.32H), 'Ubaadah ibn Saamit (d.34H), Abu Moosaa al-Ash'aree (d.44H), 'Imraan ibn Husain (d.52H), 'Ammar ibn Yaasir (d.37H), Abu Hurairah (d.57H), Hudhaifah ibn al-Yamaan (d.36H), 'Uqbah ibn 'Aamir al-Juhanee (d.58H), Salmaan (d.35H), Jaabir (d.74H), Abu Sa'eed al-Khudree (d.74H), Hudhaifah ibn Usaid al-Ghifaaree (d.42H), Abu Umaamah Sudayya ibn 'Ajlaan [al-Baahilee] (d.86H), Jundub ibn 'Abdillaah (d.64H), Abu Mas'ood 'Uqbah ibn 'Amr (d.40H), 'Umair ibn Habeeb ibn

---

1. All of the Companions, *radiallaahu 'anhum*, were *Imaams* of guidance, but there were some who were very famous, so perhaps the author only intended to mention the most famous of them or those who narrated the majority of the narrations.

Khumaashah, Abut-Tufail 'Aamir ibn Waalithah (d.110H), 'Aa'ishah (d.58H), and Umm Salamah (d.62H). *radiallaahu 'anhum ajma'een.*

From the *Taabi'een* from the People of Madeenah

Sa'eed ibn al-Musayyib (d.94H), 'Urwah ibn az-Zubayr (d.94H), al-Qaasim ibn Muhammad ibn Abee Bakr (d.106H), Saalim ibn 'Abdillaah ibn 'Umar (d.106H), Sulaimaan ibn Yassar (d.107H), Muhmmad ibn al-Hanafiyyah (d.81H), 'Alee ibn al-Husain ibn 'Alee [Zainul-'Aabideen] (d.94H), and his son Muhammad ibn 'Alee ibn Husain (d.114H), 'Umar ibn 'Abdul-'Azeez (d.101H), Ka'b ibn Maati' al-Ahbaar (d.32H) and Zaid ibn Aslam (d.136H).

From the Second Level

Muhmmad ibn Muslim, az-Zuhree (d.124H), Rabee'ah ibn 'Abdir-Rahmaan (d.136H), 'Abdullaah ibn Yazeed ibn Hurmuz, Zayd ibn 'Alee ibn al-Husain (d.122H), 'Abdullaah ibn Hasan [ibn Abee Taalib] (d.145H) and Ja'far ibn Muhammad as-Saadiq (d.148H).

From the Third Level

Abu 'Abdillaah: Maalik ibn Anas, the Faqeeh (d.179H) and 'Abdul-'Azeez ibn Abee Salamah al-Maajishoon (d.164H).

Those After Them

His son 'Abdul-Maalik ibn 'Abdul-'Azeez (d.212H), Ismaa'eel ibn Abee Uwais (d.226H) and Abu Mus'ab Ahmad ibn Abee Bakr az-Zuhree (d.292H).

From Those Counted As Being From Them

Yahyaa ibn Abee Katheer al-Yamamee (d.129H).

From the People of Makkah and Those counted Amongst Them

'Ataa' [ibn Abee Rabaah] (d.114H), Taawoos (d.106H), Mujaahid (d.103H) and Ibn Abee Mulaikah (d.117H).

Those in the Level After Them

'Amr ibn Deenaar (d.126H), 'Abdullaah ibn Taawoos (d.132H) then: Ibn Juraij (d.150H), Naafi' ibn 'Umar al-Jumahee (d.179H), Sufyaan ibn 'Uyainah (d.198H), Fudayl ibn 'Iyyad (d.187H), Muhmmad ibn Muslim at-Taa'ifee (d.177H), Yahyaa ibn Saleem at-Taa'ifee (d.195H) then: Abu 'Abdillaah Muhmmad ibn Idrees ash-Shaafi'ee, the Faqeeh (d.204H) then: 'Abdullaah ibn Yazeed al-Muqri' (d.213H) and 'Abdullaah ibn az-Zubayr al-Humaydee (d.219H). *Radiallaahu 'anhum ajma'een.*

From the People of Shaam and the Arabian Peninsula and Those Counted Amongst them - From the *Taabi'een*

'Abdullaah ibn Muhayreez (d.99H), Rajaa' ibn Haywah (d.112H), 'Ubadah ibn Nusayy (d.118H), Maymoon ibn Mihraan (d.117H) and 'Abdul-Kareem ibn Maalik al-Jazaree (d.127H).

Then Those After Them

'Abdur-Rahmaan ibn 'Amr al-Awzaa'ee (d.157H), Muhammad ibn al-Waleed az-Zubaydee (d.148H), Sa'eed ibn 'Abdil-'Azeez at-Tanookhee (d.167H), 'Abdur-Rahmaan ibn Yazeed ibn Jaabir (d.153H), and 'Abdullaah ibn Shawadhab (d.144H) and Abu

Ishaaq, Ibraaheem ibn Muhammad al-Fazaaree (d.186H).

Then Those After Them

Abu Mushir: 'Abdul-A'laa ibn Mushir ad-Dimashqee (d.218H), Hishaam ibn 'Ammaar ad-Dimashqee (d.245H) and Muhammad ibn Sulaymaan al-Misseesee, known as 'Luwayn' (d.240H).

From the People of Egypt

Haywah ibn Shuraih (d.158H), al-Layth ibn Sa'd (d.175H) and 'Abdullaah ibn Lahee'ah (d.174H).

Those After Them

'Abdullaah ibn Wahb (d.197H), Ashhab ibn 'Abdil-'Azeez (d.204H), 'Abdur-Rahmaan ibn al-Qaasim (d.191H), Abu Ibraheem, Ismaa'eel ibn Yahyaa al-Muzanee (d.264H), Abu Ya'qoob, Yoosuf ibn Yahyaa al-Buwaytee (d.231H), ar-Rabee' ibn Sulaymaan al-Muraadee (d.207H) and Muhammad ibn 'Abdillaah ibn 'Abdil-Hakam al-Misree (d.268H).

From the People of Koofah

'Alqamah ibn Qays (d.62H), 'Aamir ibn Sharaaheel ash-Sha'bee (d.104H), Abul-Bukhtaree: Sa'eed ibn Fayrooz (d.83H), Ibraaheem ibn Yazeed an-Nakhaa'ee (d.96H), Talhah ibn Musarrif (d.112H), Zubayd ibn al-Haarith (d.123H), al-Hakam ibn 'Utaybah (d.115H), Maalik ibn Mighwaal (d.159H), Abu Hayyaan Yahyaa ibn Sa'eed at-Tameemee (d.145H), 'Abdul-Maalik Ajbar, Hamzah ibn Habeeb az-Zayyaat al-Muqri' (d.156H).

Then: Muhammad ibn 'Abdir-Rahmaan ibn Abee Laylaa (d.148H), Sufyaan ath-Thawree (d.161H), Shareek ibn 'Abdillaah al-Qaadee (d.177H), Zaa'idah ibn Qudaamah (d.161H), Abu Bakr ibn 'Ayyaash (d.193), 'Abdullaah ibn Idrees (al-Awdee) (d.192H), 'Abdur-Rahmaan ibn Muhammad al-Muhaaribee (d.195H), Yahyaa ibn 'Abdil-Maalik ibn Abee Ghaniyyah (d.186H), Wakee' ibn al-Jarraah (d.197H), Abu Usaamah Hammaad ibn Usaamah (d.201H), Ja'far ibn 'Awn (d.209H), Muhammad ibn 'Ubayd at-Tanaafis (d.204H), Abu Nu'aym al-Fadl ibn Dukayn (d.219H), Ahmad ibn 'Abdillaah ibn Yoonus (al-Yarboo'ee) (d.227H), Abu Bakr ibn Abee Shaybah (d.235H), his brother 'Uthmaan (d.239H) and Abu Kurayb Muhammad ibn al-'Alaa' al-Hamdhaanee (d.248H).

From the People of Basrah

Abul-'Aaliyah Rufai' ibn Mihraan ar-Riyaahee, the freed slave of a woman of the Banoo Riyaah (d.93H), al-Hasan ibn Abil-Hasan al-Basree (d.110H), Muhammad ibn Seereen (d.110H), Abu Qilaabah 'Abdullaah ibn Zayd al-Jarmee (d.104H).

Those After them

Abu Bakr Ayyoob ibn Abee Tameemah as-Sakhtiyaanee (d.131H), Yoonus ibn 'Ubayd (d.139H), 'Abdullaah ibn 'Awn (d.151H), Sulaymaan at-Taymee (d.143H) and Abu 'Umar ibn al-'Alaa' (d.154H).

Then: Hammad ibn Salamah (d.167H), Hammad ibn Zayd (d.179H), Yahyaa ibn Sa'eed al-Qattaan (d.198H), and Mu'aadh ibn Mu'aadh (at-Tameemee) (d.196H).

Then: 'Abdur-Rahmaan ibn Mahdee (d.198H), Wahb ibn Jareer

(d.206H), Abul-Hasan 'Alee ibn 'Abdillaah ibn Ja'far al-Madeenee (d.234H), 'Abbaas ibn 'Abdil-'Adheem al-'Anbaree (d.246H), Muhammad ibn Bashshaar (Bundaar) (d.252H) and Sahl ibn 'Abdillaah at-Tustaree (d.283H).

From the People of Waasit

Hushaym ibn Basheer al-Waasitee (d.183H), 'Amr ibn 'Awn (d.225H), Shaadh ibn Yahyaa, Wahb ibn Baqiyyah (d.239H) and Ahmad ibn Sinaan (d.256H).

From the People of Baghdaad

Abu 'Abdillaah Ahmad ibn Muhammad ibn Hanbal (d.241H), Abu Zakariyyaa Yahyaa ibn Ma'een (d.233H), Abu 'Ubayd al-Qaasim ibn Sallaam (d.224H), Abu Thawr Ibraaheem ibn Khaalid al-Kalbee (d.240H), Abu Khaithamah Zuhayr ibn Ibraaheem ad-Dawraqee (d.246H), Muhammad ibn Jareer at-Tabaree (d.310H), Ahmad ibn Salmaan an-Najjaad, the *Faqeeh* (d.348H) and Abu Bakr Muhammad ibn al-Hasan an-Naqqaash al-Muqri' (d.351H).

From the People of Mawsil

Al-Ma'aafee ibn 'Imraan al-Mawsilee (d.286H).

From the People of Khurasaan

Abu 'Ubaydir-Rahmaan 'Abdullaah ibn al-Mubaarak al-Marwazee (d.181H), al-Fadl ibn Moosaa as-Seenaanee (d.192H), an-Nadr ibn Muhammad al-Marwazee (d.183H), an-Nadr ibn Shumayl al-Maazinee (d.203H), Nu'aym ibn Hammaad al-Marwazee (d.229H), Ishaaq ibn Ibraaheem ibn Makhlad, known as Ibn Raahooyah al-Marwazee (d.238H), Ahmad ibn Sayyaar al-Marwazee (d.268H),

Muhammad ibn Nasr al-Marwazee (d.238H), Yahyaa ibn Yahyaa an-Neesaabooree (d.226H), Muhammad ibn Yahyaa adh-Dhuhlee (d.258H), Muhammad ibn Aslam at-Toosee (d.242H), Humayd ibn Zanjawaih an-Nasawee (d.249H), Abu Qudaamah 'Ubaydullaah ibn Sa'eed as-Sarkhas (d.241H), 'Abdullaah ibn 'Abdir-Rahman as-Samarqandee (ad-Daarimee) (d.250H), Muhammad ibn Ismaa'eel al-Bukhaaree (d.256H), Ya'qoob ibn Sufyaan al-Fasawee (d.277H), Abu Daawood Sulaymaan ibn al-Ash'ath as-Sijjistaanee who settled in Basrah (d.275H), Abu 'Abdir-Rahmaan an-Nasawee (Imaam an-Nasaa'ee) (d.303H), Abu 'Eesaa Muhammad ibn 'Eesaa at-Tirmidhee (d.279H) and Muhammad ibn 'Aqeel al-Balkee (d.316H).

From the People of Rayy

Ibraaheem ibn Moosaa al-Farraa' (d. after 220H), Abu Zur'ah 'Ubaydullaah ibn 'Abdil-Kareem ar-Raazee (d.264H), Abu Haatim Muhammad ibn Idrees al-Hanzaalee (d.277H), Abu 'Ubaydillaah Muhammad ibn Waarah (d.270H) and Abu Mas'ood Ahmad ibn al-Furaat, who settled in Asbahaan (d.258H).

After Them

'Abdur-Rahmaan ibn Abee Haatim (d.328H).

From the People of Tabaristaan

Ismaa'eel ibn Sa'eed ash-Shaalanjee (d.230 or 246H), al-Husayn ibn 'Alee at-Tabaree, Abu Nu'aym 'Abdul-Maalik ibn 'Adiyy al-Istiraabaadhee (d.288H) and 'Alee ibn Ibraaheem al-Qattaan al-Qazweenee (d.345H).

INDEX

Index of Sects

The Sect	Number of the Point Covering it
Ahl us-Sunnah wal-Jamaa'ah	3
Jabariyyah, Jabaree	141
Jahmiyyah, Jahmee	50, 84, 97, 98, 99, 100, 123, 141, 146, 157
Khawaarij, Khaarijee	33, 35, 159
Mujbirah, Mujbir	141
Murji'ah, Murji'ee	159
Mu'tazilah, Mu'tazilee	141, 146
Nawaasib, Naasibee	141
Qadariyyah, Qadaree	141, 159
Rawaafid, Raafidee	141, 146, 161
Shee'ah, Shee'ee	159, 161

Note: The first name in the above index denotes the name of the sect, whilst the second name denotes a follower of that sect. The terms *Jabariyyah* and *Mujbirah* denote the same sect.

Subject Index

Glossary

Aayah (pl. Aayaat): A sign of Allaah; a number of His words occurring together in the Qur'aan.

Ahl us-Sunnah wal-Jamaa'ah: Those who remain upon that which the Prophet (ﷺ) and his Companions were upon with regards to *'Aqeedah*, methodology and all matters of the Religion, not leaving their way in favour of the ways of the innovated sects such as the *Raafidees*, the *Khawaarij*, the *Mu'tazilah*, the *Ash'arees* and the *Maatureedees*.

'Alaihis-salaam: "May Allaah, the One free from all defects, protect and preserve him." It is said after the name of a Prophet of Allaah or after the name of any angel.

Ansaar: "Helpers"; the Muslims of Madeenah who supported the Muslims who migrated from Makkah.

'Aqeedah: The principles and details of belief.

Bid'ah: Innovation; anything introduced into the Religion, in order to seek Allaah's pleasure, not having a specific proof or basis in the Religion.

Deenaar: unit of currency in the Arab lands.

Dirham: unit of currency in the Arab lands.

Du'aa: Invocation; supplication.

Eemaan: Correct Islamic Faith comprising belief of the heart, saying with the tongue and actions of the limbs. It can increase and decrease.

Fiqh: The understanding and application of the *Sharee'ah* from its sources.

Hadeeth (pl. Ahaadeeth): A narration concerning the utterances of the Prophet (ﷺ), his actions or an attribute of his.

Haafidhahullaah: May Allaah protect him.

Hanbalee: One well-versed in the *fiqh* passed on by the students of Imaam Ahmad ibn Hanbal.

Hasan: A good and acceptable *hadeeth*.

Hijrah: The emigration of the Prophet (ﷺ) from Makkah to al-Madeenah; migration of the Muslims from the lands of the disbelievers to the lands of the Muslims.

Iblees: Shaitaan, the accursed.

Ijmaa': Consensus.

Imaam: Leader; leader in Prayer, knowledge or *fiqh*; leader of a state.

Isnaad: The chain of narration of a *hadeeth* (i.e. so and so narrated to me from so and so...).

Jamaa'ah: The united body of the Muslims, together upon the truth, i.e. the Companions and those who remain upon their way.

Janaazah: Funeral rites.

Jihaad: Striving and fighting to make the Word of Allaah supreme.

Kaafir: A disbeliever.

Khaleefah (pl. Khulafaa'): The leader of the Muslim *Ummah*.

Khutbah: An Islamic address (e.g. the *khutbah* of *Jumu'ah*).

Kufr: Disbelief.

Kunyah: The title Abu (father of so and so) or Umm (mother of so and so).

Qiblah: The direction one faces during Prayer (i.e. towards Makkah).

Manhaj: The methodology of the Muslim; the way, method and outlook he holds to.

Marfoo': A *hadeeth* attributed to the Prophet (ﷺ).

Muhaajir: One who does *hijrah*.

Muhaddith: A scholar of the science of *hadeeth*.

Mujaahid: One who does *jihaad*.

Mushaf: The printed Qur'aan.

Mushrik: One who attributes partners to Allaah.

Mutawaatir: A *hadeeth* reported by a large number of narrators at every stage of its transmission, so that it is impossible that it could have been invented. Scholars differ about the minimum number of narrators needed to constitute a *mutawaatir hadeeth*.

Radiallaahu 'anhu/'anha/'anhum/'anhummaa: May Allaah be pleased with him/her/them/both of them.

Rahimahullaah: May Allaah have mercy upon him.

Rahmatullaah 'alaihimaa: May Allaah have mercy upon both of them.

Rak'ah: One unit of Prayer.

Saheeh: Authentic; a *hadeeth* fulfilling all the conditions of authenticity.

Salaf: Predecessors; the early Muslims; the Muslims of the first three generations: the Companions, the Successors and their successors.

Salaam: The prescribed greetings of the Muslims: *assalaamu 'alaikum...* (May Allaah preserve and protect you...).

Shaikh: Scholar.

Sharee'ah: The Divine code of law.

Shirk: Associating partners with Allaah.

Soorah: A chapter of the Qur'aan.

Sunnah: In its broadest sense the entire religion which the Prophet (ﷺ) came with i.e. all matters of beliefs, rulings, manners ad actions which were conveyed by the Companions. It also includes those matters which the Prophet (ﷺ) established by his sayings, actions and tacit approval.

Taabi'ee (pl. Taabi'een): "The Successors"; The successors of the Companions.

Taabi' ut-Taabi'een: The successors of the successors of the Companions.

Tafseer: Explanation (of the Qur'aan).

Takbeer: *"Allaahu akbar."* (Allaah is greater).

Tawaaf: Circling the Ka'bah seven times as an act of worship.

Ummah: The Muslim nation.

Zakaah: Charity that is an obligation on anyone who has wealth over and above a certain limit over which a year has passed.

Zuhd: Abstinence from the alluring things of this world.

Bibliography of English Works

The following works have been mentioned in the notes as useful reading material where indicated:

'Abdul-Hameed, A.H. (1994) *Death (transl.)*. Al-Hidaayah: Birmingham.

Al-Albaanee, M.N. (1993), *The Prophet's Prayer Described (transl.)*. Al-Haneef Publications: Ipswich.

Al-Munajjid, M.S. (1993) *I Would Like to Repent, But! (transl.)*. Iqra Welfare Trust: Bangalore, India.

As-Sabt, A. (1994) *Prayer in Congregation (transl.)*. Dar of Islamic Heritage: USA.

As-Sabt, A. (1994) *The Ever-Merciful Istiwaa Over the Throne (transl.)*. Dar of Islamic Heritage: USA.

Hasan, S. (1988) *Faith in Predestination (transl.)*. Al-Quran Society: London.

Khan, M.M. (1984) *Sahih Al-Bukhari (transl.)*. Kitab Bhavan: New Delhi.

Philips, A.A.B. (1990) *Fundamentals of Tawheed*. Tawheed Publications: Riyadh.

Philips, A.A.B. (1990) *Salvation Through Repentance*. Tawheed Publications: Riyadh.

Philips, A.A.B. (1987) *The Mirage in Iran*. Tawheed Publications: New York.

Philips, A.A.B. (1985) *The Devils Deception of the Shee'ah (transl.)*. As Suq Bookstore: New York.

Siddiqi, A.H. (1990) *Sahih Muslim (transl.)*. Sh. Muhammad Ashraf: Lahore.

Zaheer, I.E. *Shias and the House of Ali (transl.)*. Idara Tarjamun Al-Sunnah: Lahore.

Zaheer, I.E. *The Shiites and the Sunnah (transl.)*. Idara Tarjamun Al-Sunnah: Lahore.